BILLY D.
AN AMERICAN
HER

BILLY D.

AN AMERICAN
HER★

by MARK DAVID KASPER

www.hispubg.com
A division of HISpecialists, llc

Inquiries should be addressed to HIS Publishing Group,
PO Box 12516, Dallas, Texas 75225.

Published by HIS Publishing Group, a Division
of Human Improvement Specialists, llc
Contact: info@hispubg.com

Cover by Haedon Design Studios
Edited by Libby York Stauder
Interior Design by Anton Khodakovsky

Library of Congress Control Number: 2012913547
ISBN: 978-0-578-10521-5

Printed and bound in the United States of America

DEDICATION

To the courageous men who sacrificed their lives for our freedom

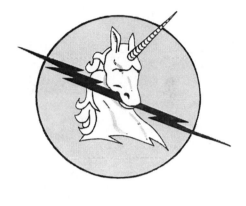

359th
Fighter Group

368th
Fighter Squadron

Acknowledgements

*I wish to thank Char Baldridge, the 359th fighter group historian,
for the courtesy of her help and the photos she provided so generously.
I also wish to thank Larry Kasper, my brother, for providing
the Department of Defense declassified documents and Dad's log book.*

RESOURCES

I would like to extend a Special Thank You to the following who provided input so Dad's story could be told.

Billy D. Kasper (dad)

Phyllis (Phyl) Mae Kasper (mother)

Thelma A. Kasper (dad's mother)

Steve Kasper (brother)—produced video recounting dad's life

Shirley May Keifor (dad's cousin)

Johnny Carter, Junior (Leonard Carter's nephew)

Joann Hovden Gardner (Lester Hovden's loving sister)

359th Fighter Group 1943-1945 reprinted by The Battery Press

The 359th Fighter Group in World War Two, Kent D. Miller

359th Fighter Group, Jack H. Smith

Jigger Tinplate & Red Cross

Mustangs & Unicorns: A History of the 359th FG, Jack H. Smith

The people at The Eighth Air Force Museum in Savannah, Georgia

T. P. Smith—370th Fighter Squadron Pilot who also provided photographs taken in East Wretham

PRELUDE

I f my father knew that I was writing a book about him, he would probably ask, "Why would you write about me?" Dad was a humble man. He did not envy what others had—on the contrary. He delighted and shared in his friends' excitement over the purchase of a new gun, car, house, etc. He was honest and true to his word. He was a gentleman. He was a man's man. He loved to laugh and he loved to spend time with his family.

A friend of Dad's and Mom's once told me, "Don't get me wrong, I loved my husband very much, but your father was the best man I ever knew."

Dad didn't have a lot of money, a big house, or expensive clothes or cars. He was, however, the richest man I ever knew.

The events of the following story are true to the best of my knowledge. Four names have been changed: Joey, Mr. & Mrs. Bob, and Aspane, because no one could remember the actual names. My apologies. This is the story of the life of my father, Billy D. Kasper. It was written by my hand. The story is told from my father's point of view. Mom said I did a pretty good job. During the course of our lifetime our minds create a photo album filled with snapshots of our life experiences. The following is my attempt to recreate my father's mental album using words, phrases, and stories told by Dad.

MY YOUTH

HARVEY, ILLINOIS

My name is Billy David Kasper. Don't call me William, or Ma will sharply correct you, "His name is *Billy!*"

I was born August 7, 1923, in Harvey, Illinois, a suburb of Chicago. Chicago was a busy city filled with tall buildings, trolley cars, and smoky automobiles. The old coexisted with the new—horse-drawn buggies and wagons were still commonplace. The giant stockyards (Chicago's first industry) still employed a great many people. Chicago, the modern city, had industry and manufacturing, banking and futures markets, shipping and enormous rail yards to ship and receive goods. It was a bustling metropolis. Stores were stocked with goods from all over the world. Chicago catered to its citizens' shopping appetites with stores like Marshall Fields.

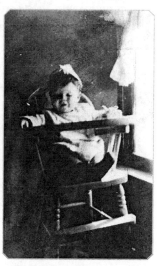

Billy D. at six months

Chicago was a fun place to visit. It had the Wrigley Building, which was 32 stories tall and right on Michigan Avenue. There was also the Tribune Tower, with stones in its entrance from Westminster Abby, Cologne

Cathedral, the Alamo, the Taj Mahal, the Great Pyramids, and the Arc de Triomphe. The stones kind of connected you to some of the most fantastic places in the world. If I tried hard enough, my imagination could take me to one of those faraway places. There was also the Buckingham Fountain, which shot water 135 feet high. I would lose myself—mouth open and eyes wide as saucers. WOW! I could stand and stare at it all day.

In the 1920s, women wore knee-length dresses to show off their legs. Some even wore dresses that allowed the male eye to see a nipple and imagine the form of the breast. Floppy hats and short hairdos were in. Women had won the right to vote in 1920, but I didn't care about all that stuff. I was a kid.

Well-off men wore top hats and tuxedos when they went out on the town in their chauffeur-driven automobiles. Men were leaving the farm and moving to towns to work in the shops and factories. After WWI, the United States emerged as an industrial and military power. There were good-paying jobs in modern American cities. The United States really *arrived* in the 20th century! We were a country that could make a difference... influence world policy. That is pretty heady stuff for a one-hundred-plus-year-old country. Ready or not, we were a player on a very large stage. We had fascists, communists, and anarchists. You name them, we had them. But, again, I was just a kid. I didn't understand that stuff.

Doc Bradley delivered brothers Billy D. (1923) and Richard L. (1933)

Harvey was on the South Side of Chicago at 157th Street. The city had a population of about 12,000 people. Harvey had paved streets and cement sidewalks. It had a nice little downtown with a couple of banks and the pride of Harvey—Thornton Township High School. Harvey even had a hospital, although I was never in it. I was born at home. If I ever needed to be sewn up or checked out, Ma took me down the street to Doc Bradley's. We lived in a modern era, but some of the old ways hung on.

My mom was 19 years old when she had me. Her name was Thelma, but I called her Mother, Ma, or Mom. She would always say that she and I grew up together. She was a good mom. She took care of me. She was a tough old bird, though, and sometimes she was hard on me...probably because I deserved it. I was all boy. Kind of a street-wise kid, but I had fun and a good childhood.

My father's name was Frank. He was a couple years older than Ma, and didn't like to discipline me. He did, but Ma took care of most of the discipline. I do remember hearing, "Wait till your father gets home!" Sometimes he did blister my bottom, but all in all, he was a gentle teacher and parent. Hell, if I so much as got a cut he would practically faint. Needless to say, when I was a child, my father must have been dizzy a lot.

Billy D. at age 4 on tricycle

As I said, Ma handed out most of the discipline, but she had a soft and caring side, too. When she was a little girl, her best friend died. Ma and her friend played together and shared secrets and giggles, as little girls do. One evening, Ma's friend was walking down the stairs of her home. It was dark, so she held a kerosene lantern to light her way. She stepped on the hem of her nightgown, stumbled, and fell down the stairs. The lamp shattered, the kerosene spilled out, and the flames engulfed her. She cried out, and her parents rushed to put out the fire. Unfortunately, they were too late and she died soon after. Ma would go to her grave to weed it and put flowers on it. She took care of her friend's grave up until the day we moved to Philadelphia. No one probably tends that little girl's grave anymore.

My dad was a great man who taught me a lot. He liked to know how things worked; I liked to know how things worked. He was a Master Mechanic; I became a Master Mechanic. He told me that the first engine he ever tore down and rebuilt had some leftover parts. He didn't know where the parts went, but the damned thing ran. When my father and I would drive around town he would give me—well, safety lessons. "You see that fella with the patch on his eye, Billy? When you work around equipment, you have to be careful of it...and the guys you are working with. That man was bleeding air out of a brake line. The fella helping him pushed on the pedal when he wasn't ready and the brake fluid sprayed right in his eye. He's lucky he didn't lose both eyes." Or my father would say, "You know Jim Jones? He was working on his car and for some reason the engine was running and he got his hand caught in the fan blade. Don't get near belts, pulleys, or fan blades when the engine is running." And sometimes Dad would say, "When you jack up a car, make sure you block it so you don't get squished. A car can roll when it's up on a jack."

Dad worked for a company called Buda that built gasoline-, diesel-, and natural gas-powered engines. These big, powerful engines helped to power America. They were used by Marion Shovel, which produced excavating and mining equipment, and also powered International Harvester trucks and Fleet Tractors. These engines could be found in everything from fishing boats to powering generators that ran ice cream plants or corn grinders.

When my father wasn't at Buda building and testing engines, he was fixing the neighbor's trucks and automobiles. I would hang over the fender and watch him work. I'd hand him tools and even work a wrench when I got older. I can remember Dad working on a truck engine in the freezing cold. I stood on a box and leaned over the fender. In my hand was rolled up newspapers. Dad lit the papers and I held the flame to the intake manifold while he turned over the old diesel. Diesels could be tough to start on a cold winter day. The newspaper torch would warm the air as it was sucked in to the engine through the manifold. An engine needs air and fuel. The intake manifold provides air to the engine.

Speaking of cold, Chicago sure could get cold in the winter. The wind would blow off of Lake Michigan and would cut right through you. Everywhere I went I was cold. Outdoors or indoors, there was no escaping the deep freeze of a Chicago winter day. I don't think they had invented insulation yet...or it they had, it hadn't made it to our house. We had a coal-fired gravity furnace, which relied on the principle that heat rises. The furnace had no blower motors to force hot air throughout the house via ducts. The heat radiated through large grates in the floor. Not very efficient.

I would lie in my bed at night, covers piled on, wearing my long-johns. I was still cold as hell. My teeth chattered until I thought they would fall out or break off. Poor Father would get up early and stoke the furnace. Whenever he could, he came home from work at lunch to eat and shovel coal.

In the summer, Chicago was hot. You could fry an egg on the sidewalk. Air-conditioning hadn't made its way into our house. It was available, but who could afford it? We had fans, but on hot summer days there was no relief. A person could not afford to buy enough ice blocks to stay cool. I can remember sweating morning till night. Sometimes, we would go to the Calumet River to cool off, or Father would drive us to Lake Michigan. The only problem was, I couldn't swim. I didn't like to be in the water, but if you get hot enough—in you go.

I remember lying in bed at night, just dripping in sweat. I would lie in one spot and it would become drenched. I'd roll to a dry spot and hunt for a dry corner of my pillow. It seemed that no matter what I did, I was lying on an uncomfortable, wet sheet. The summers were miserable and the winters were unbearable. Maybe it was the cold winters and hot summers that made me appreciate spring and fall so much.

Growing up in Harvey was fun. I always had something to do, and almost all of our family lived there. Grandpa (Jack) Kasper and Grandma (Marguerite Wheat) Kasper lived on the north end of Harvey. Dad was their oldest child, and he had two brothers who lived with Grandma and Grandpa. One brother was named Dick, and he opened a butcher shop shortly before the Depression. When the Depression came along, meat was rationed. That was the end of the butcher shop. He later found a little store near downtown Chicago and bought it cheap. He had a little deli, and Grandma would make donuts to sell on the weekends. Dick had a good personality. He could laugh at anyone's jokes. He really liked people and made a good living. He worked at that store until he retired.

Dad's other brother was Wayne. Wayne worked as a welder and put himself through school. He graduated from Northwestern University and became an accountant. Father's sister, Henrietta, married a fella by the name of Swift. They moved to Wisconsin and started a family.

Grandpa Kasper was a barber. He could also cut meat or do carpentry work. He told me, "Billy, a man should always have three trades. That way, if hard times come, you always have something to fall back on." I thought

Grandpa was the smartest man I ever knew. I loved him very much.

Grandpa moved to Harvey from Sandusky in northwestern Ohio. I was told that he worked and saved his money until he had enough money to go back east and claim his wife. He traveled to Indiana and expressed his love for Marguerite, promising her father that he would provide for her and be a good husband. They married,

Store in Harvey, Illinois 1912—John Kasper (far left) and brother-in-law Frank Wheat (third from left)

moved to Chicago, and raised a family.

When Grandpa didn't have a customer, he'd give me a haircut and shave—not a real shave. I was just a kid. He would set me up in the chair and put the warm shaving cream on me. Boy, did it feel good! Then, he would sharpen his razor on the strap. Next, using a finger and the backside of the razor, he would scrape off the shaving cream. Finally, he would wipe my face with a warm towel. I sure felt grown up when Grandpa gave me a shave.

Grandpa's barber shop was a fun place to hang out. Men would come into the shop and talk about stuff that a small boy didn't understand, like politics and business and current events. I not only got to see Grandpa, but his Airedale Terrier was almost always there. I would play and run with him. He would find his way to my house, sneak in by nosing the door open, and run into my room. Then, he'd jump up on my bed, muddy paws and all, and lick me till I was awake and laughing. Ma would chase that dog off my bed and out into the yard, where he would wait until I came out to play. I loved that dog.

Sometimes, Grandpa would have a customer who couldn't pay for a shave and haircut. He might trade a haircut for tools, food, a gun, or anything else that might interest Grandpa. Trading was one way that Grandpa added to his gun collection. He had a big gun collection. Sometimes, he would give me a broken gun and I would take it home.

When Ma saw it, she would hit the roof. "You take that right back to Jack Kasper!" she'd holler. Then, she would raise hell with Grandpa. "Don't give that boy anymore guns. A little boy has no need for a gun."

Grandpa would say, "Okay, Thelma, no more guns." I think Grandpa had a short memory.

My mother was a Schooley. She had one half-brother. He was a Bailey. I never knew my Grandpa Schooley. Grandma (Edna Mae) Bailey would have had a fit if he had ever come around. Not because he was a bad person, but because she was...different. I don't know how anyone could live with her. Grandma Bailey was gruff, surly, harsh, and unsmiling. I can say this for her, though—she had pretty chestnut hair and a nice singing voice.

Grandma divorced twice and buried husband number two. Three husbands and two children from those marriages. When Ma was just a baby, Grandma left Grandpa Schooley. She carried Ma and followed the railroad tracks to her mother's house. She walked 10 miles with Mom. Grandpa was forbidden to come around and see his daughter. He did try to keep an eye on her and watch her grow up. Sometimes, when Mother would walk home from school, she would smell cigar smoke in the air. She would look around and there he'd be, tall and thin, wearing a suit and straw hat. He would smile and nod to Ma. Mother would nod back and smile and then hurry on home. She knew if she got caught anywhere near Grandpa, she would get skinned alive.

When Ma was older, she was out late one night. Wouldn't you know it, her father was there.

"You're out late, aren't you?" he asked.

"What business is it of yours?" Thelma replied.

Grandpa didn't respond. He just turned and walked away. Mom always regretted that.

My mother's younger half-brother was named Raymond Bailey. Raymond was a tall, good-looking man with wavy hair. Every now and then, he would get into a scrape. I think a lot of times it was over some woman. Raymond was a ladies' man, and he was always into something.

Prohibition had come to America in the 1920s. One time, don't ask me why, Father went to a speakeasy with Raymond. They walked up to the bar and Raymond ordered whiskeys for the two of them.

They both drank their drinks and Father looked at Raymond. Raymond got tightlipped and said, "Watered down." His eyes glared and he called the bartender over. The bartender approached Raymond, and POW! Raymond laid him out. Father sat there, eyes wide and jaw dropped. Father and Raymond then walked out quickly.

All the while, Father was saying, "Why the hell did you do a thing like that, Raymond?"

"A man that serves watered-down booze deserves that," said Raymond.

I don't think Father went to any more speakeasies with Raymond.

Grandma Bailey and I didn't really get along. Even when I was little, I liked to aggravate her. I would go off and hide, and she would look in every room of the house for me, but no Bill. She would go outside and check around the house, but no Bill. She knew I wouldn't go very far, so she would stand outside and call in a pleasant singing voice, "Billy, Billy…" Then, her tone would change.

When she hollered my whole name, I knew I was getting to her. "Billy David Kasper, you answer me!" I knew she was at her wit's end when she said, "Billy, you come here this instant or I'm going to give you away to the gypsies."

Finally, my giggling would give me away. Then, I would really get it. I just never liked Grandma.

When I was a small boy, walking around in my knickers, I enjoyed life, but something was missing. I wanted a baby brother. Mother would say that Doc Bradley was in charge of the "baby department." I would go in the house and get my old baby carriage. Then, down the street I'd go—right to Doc Bradley's. I'd march up to his door and knock on it. Doc would open up and ask what he could do for me.

"I want a baby brother. I want you to put a baby in that carriage for me."

Doc Bradley would laugh at my requests and say, "Billy, you need to go home and ask your mother and father to put a baby in that carriage."

I didn't get it. I thought I was getting the runaround. Doc Bradley brought me and all the other kids into this world. How were Mother and Father supposed to do his job?

At the age of six I had my first run-in with a car. I ran across the street just as an old Ford rounded the corner. He clipped my leg, and the force of the impact tossed me head first into the curb. The man got out of his car to see if I was all right. I had quite a bruise on my head, but I was okay. Doc Bradley looked me over and pronounced me fit. I was a good customer of Doc Bradley's. He sewed me up and tended to all of my bumps and cuts.

Billy D. at age six

Another traumatic incident occurred when I was six. I was force marched into the first grade. I didn't want to go to school. I had no use for it, and besides, I was having too much fun to let school get in the way. Mother said that all little boys and girls my age had to go to school. She said I would learn to read, write, and do arithmetic. I asked Ma to teach me, but she said that she was a mother, not a teacher. I grudgingly agreed to go to school, but I asked if I could quit in a couple of years like Father had. Ma told me that Father was forced to quit school to help the family. He was 13 when he went to work in the onion fields. I don't know what kind of work he did, but it was hard work. Marguerite made him turn over every nickel he made—he didn't get to keep one cent. As a matter of fact, Father never learned to keep too many cents. When he and Ma got married, Ma had to pay for the marriage license. She also bought their first car.

Anyway, off to school I went. I attended Whittier Elementary School from grades one through eight. I attended first grade twice. Miss Way failed me. She told Mother that I didn't pay attention and all I did was stare out the window. I had better things to do, like fighting the Germans in WWI.

I had a little toy biplane. I remember sitting on the pot, shooting down Germans with that plane. I was a triple ace...at *least*. My dream was to be a flying ace. An aerial gentleman with a scarf and high leather boots. I guess my head was in the clouds.

I did better the second time around in first grade, and was never held back again. I learned to play the clarinet. Instruments were cheap back then, so Mom and Dad didn't mind buying me one. Our school had a good band, and we took first in the state. I even got a first place in a woodwind quartet. When I graduated high school I put the clarinet down and never picked it up again.

I made some really good friends in school. There was Louis Stubs, Harvey Goodwine, Billy Seimers, and Charles Armington. We would play kick the can and hide-n-seek. One day we went to the store and got an old orange crate. We attached skates to the crate and nailed a two-by-four to the crate to make a handle. Now we had a scooter that we took turns riding up and down the street.

One good thing about school—I learned to read. I would do any odd jobs I could to make money so I could buy paperback books about WWI flying aces. WOW! I would imagine myself with goggles on and a scarf around my neck. "Yes, sir, I'll go get the Red Baron for you, sir." There was an airport near Harvey. Whenever I heard the sound of a plane I would run up and down the street searching the sky for the approaching airplane.

I was raised during the Great Depression. We were lucky. My father always had a job. Mother didn't work. Watching over me was like having two jobs. We didn't have much money, but I didn't know it. My mother and father didn't talk about money—at least, not when I was around. I was a kid. I had a roof over my head and food to eat. I didn't have a lot of toys or other stuff, but I was happy. I didn't know what a "depression" was.

My father fixed up an old bike and gave it to me. It was great. I rode it around Harvey. I rode down to and along the Calumet River, and I'd make the three- or four-mile ride out to the airport, where there was a beautiful biplane. At first, I admired that plane from the road, then I just couldn't take it anymore. I rode up to within a few feet of it. I parked my bike and walked up to the plane. The pilot was nowhere in sight, so I walked closer to her. WOW! I was drooling.

"Get out of there, boy!" the pilot suddenly growled.

"I just wanted to see her up close, sir."

"You just stay away, boy."

I could only watch that son-of-a-bitch fly 'Miss Dixie' from a distance. His sweet disposition couldn't keep me away. Well, it did, but I still watched every chance I got. He was an S.O.B., but I couldn't get enough of that airplane.

April 24, 1931, was one of the saddest days of my life. Grandpa Kasper was 59 years old when he died. I was seven. I didn't think Grandpa would ever die. My father sat on the edge of my bed and told me that Grandpa had died. I didn't cry...maybe I was in shock. Life without my grandpa never occurred to me. It was difficult to understand that I would never again see Grandpa. There would be no more visits to his shop. No more broken guns to take home.

I don't know if it was Wayne, Dick, or both, but someone took the Airedale out to the garage. They started the engine of the car and locked the dog in the garage. He went to sleep and never woke up. It took a long time for me to forgive them. I don't know if I ever understood why they did it. Grandma sold my grandpa's gun collection. I was given his pump-action .22-caliber rifle. It would be my only reminder of him.

On Saturdays, Mom and Dad and I would go to the movies. Yes, they were talkies. Silent films were still around, but they were more of a cheap curiosity for a kid like me. I liked movies with sound. Back then, before the movie started, the theaters featured news reels with pictures of real events going on in the world. That was almost as good as the movie—no, it wasn't. I looked forward to movie day.

Things were different when I was a kid. We would get in fights at the drop of a hat, but we didn't use clubs or bottles. We weren't out to kill or maim each other. Hell, after a good fight you'd shake hands...you might even become best friends. My friends and I had a code of conduct:

> Don't pick a fight, finish a fight.
> Never pick on a little or weak guy you know you could whoop.
> No two on one, don't gang up. That's chicken shit.

No clubs, bottles, or kicking.

Never hit a man when he's down.

Don't spit—unless you just coughed up something bad.

Shake hands after a good fight.

Be honest, even if it hurts. Sometimes Ma made it hurt.

Play fair.

Don't brag.

If you gotta fart, make it a good one.

Down the street from our house was a Methodist church. Mother and Father did not go to church, but Mother did have a Bible. It was not just for decoration—she read it. On Sundays I would watch people go into church. They all had on their best suits. As they entered the church, the men took their Sunday hats off. It's not polite to wear a hat indoors. That rule is only for men, though. The women wore nice dresses with bows. They had large matching hats and wore white gloves. I'd sit outside and listen to the music. I could even hear the preacher from where I was sitting. I asked Ma if I could take myself to church. She said that that would be a fine thing for me to do. My mother and father never came to church with me and I never asked.

I got baptized and confirmed. I became a member and I always tried to put my ten percent in the collection plate. I always felt a man's giving was a measure of his worth. By the time I became a teenager I thought that someday I would become a minister. I studied my Bible and prayed real hard. I wasn't worried about my relationship with God, even though I liked a good fight. David was good in a fight and God sure loved him.

January 29, 1933, I went to church. When I got home, I had a baby brother, Richard Leo Kasper. I was nine-and-a-half years old. Doc Bradley or Mom and Dad finally put a baby in the carriage. I was so excited to have a baby brother. I loved him as much as a boy can love a brother. You know, I didn't even know Ma was pregnant. I thought she was putting on weight, but it wouldn't be polite to say anything. And besides, Richie was born in the winter and those extra clothes helped hide the baby.

In 1933, two big things, besides Richard, happened in Chicago. Mayor Cermak was shot and killed while riding in a car with president-elect

Roosevelt. "Gangsters," the paper said. Then, in the spring, Chicago opened the World's Fair. This fair highlighted inventions and life in a modern world.

Father put us all in the car, even little Richard, and we drove up to the fair. My eyes were as wide as saucers. It was wall-to-wall people. The buildings were grand and kind of futuristic. The exhibits were jaw-dropping great. There were people there lifting tremendous weights and twisting themselves into pretzels. I even saw a man wrestle an alligator! WOW! There were so many different foods. It was almost too much for a boy to take in. It was a new bold world. The world had come to Chicago...my backyard.

Billy D. at age ten and his brother Richard at 6 months

As I mentioned, I was always hanging over a fender, helping my dad fix cars and trucks. When Dad worked for Buda, he traveled a lot. After I turned eleven, I began to travel with him to be his helper. I loved working with my dad. I thought he could fix anything. I wanted to be just like him when I grew up. I learned all about engines and learned to identify good sounds and bad sounds.

"Listen to that, Billy. What do you think?"

I turned my ear to the engine. I walked around it and cocked my head to pick up all of the sounds. Then I walked to the exhaust pipe and placed my hand to feel the pulse of the engine. "Number four cylinder is losing combustion, Dad."

"That's what I think, too, Billy. Let's tear it down."

I think traveling with Dad got me out of Mother's hair. She could concentrate on Richard. I got to learn the engine trade.

After Richard was born, Mom read a book about child rearing. It was like she had a Billy switch and a Richard switch. We were raised differently—even more so after she read the book. If Richard wanted to eat dessert before his meal, then he did. If he made a mess, it was okay. If Richie threw a fit, Ma would talk to him in this sweet, soft, high-pitched voice.

A couple years after Richard was born, Shirley May Bailey was born. She was Mom's brother Raymond's little girl. Raymond had settled down (temporarily) and married Alice Trawynski. Mom, Dad, Richard, and I were very close to Shirley May. She was a good kid and had a great time with us. Up until she graduated high school, she would spend several weeks with us each summer. Mom really enjoyed having a girl in the house. I think Ma thought she and Shirley May were a lot alike. Shirley May wasn't afraid to get her hands dirty, either. She would tag along with Frank, hand him a wrench, or just keep him company.

Raymond didn't turn out to be a very good father or husband. Raymond only seemed to care about Raymond. Around this same time, Grandma Bailey divorced Mr. Bailey and moved in with us. Oh, brother! Ma really was an angel, after all. She had to be to let Grandma live with us, or else she had a screw loose. Frank was easy to get along with. If it ever bothered him that Grandma lived with us, I never knew it. Grandma Bailey made no secret of the fact that she didn't care for Frank. She thought Mother could have done better. Even knowing Grandma's feelings, Frank still allowed her to live with us.

One day, Richard and Shirley May were outside playing. Richard was five and Shirley May was three. They decided to do a little drawing. The two budding artists used a nail for their medium. Their canvas was Dad's car. Ma discovered them putting the finishing touches on their masterpiece. She sweetly said, "No, no, children, that will hurt the car." Then she hollered to Dad, "Frank, you are going to have to get your car repainted."

That was it. No punishment, whatsoever. I thought, "Who the hell stole my mother and put this woman in her place?" I still got walloped and hollered at, but it was kind of comforting in a way to know that Ma was still in that woman's body. I never held it against Ma—the way she treated Rich, that is. I know she loved me and everybody has different needs. You can't treat everyone the same. Besides, it's tough to know the right way to raise a kid. I turned out okay and Richie turned out okay, so I think that all that psychological stuff that these doctors and experts write is, well, just stuff.

Traveling with Dad was fun and exciting. The time we spent together made our relationship change. He was my father, but he was also a friend and a co-worker. I grew up a lot because of those experiences. We traveled all over...to Ohio, Idaho, Iowa, and Wisconsin, as well as other parts of Illinois.

I remember working on an engine with Dad in Idaho. That engine powered a corn grinder. In the rural areas of the United States there was no electricity, except what was powered by engines like the ones Buda produced. It was while I was traveling with my father that I began calling him Frank. Dad said, "We are two men working on a job. Two men working together call each other by their first name. So, Billy, you can call me Frank."

From then on, it was, "Hand me that open 7/16 wrench, Billy."

"Here you go, Frank."

One time, we went up to the docks at Lake Michigan in Chicago. We repaired a diesel on a fishing boat. The captain didn't want it to break down while he was in the middle of the Great Lakes, so Frank and I sailed out with them to test the engines. The engines performed perfectly.

We sailed out so far I could hardly make out the Chicago skyline. The captain ordered the nets dropped and we trolled for fish. He brought up the nets full of fish. The men worked quickly to hoist the nets in and drop the fish in the hold. We turned toward home and as we sailed, they repeated the process until the hold was full. The combination of fish smell and the bobbing up and down of the boat made my stomach feel a little funny. Then my throat felt full and my breathing was heavy. My cheeks puffed out when I exhaled and my stomach swirled. It was as if whatever was in my stomach went round and round, higher and higher, and then I was at the rail puking my guts out. I heaved and heaved. My eyes watered as I watched my puke float on the water and fish came up and fed on it. Then I puked some more. The fishermen roared with laughter as I stood there at the rail. I was very entertaining, I guess.

Seeing how sick I was, Frank suddenly dove to the rail and lost his lunch. A funny thing happened. After Frank got sick, I felt better. The rest of the trip back, Frank was miserable. I was smiling and really enjoying myself. When Frank wasn't getting sick, he was sitting, face pale and drawn, staring straight ahead at nothing.

Another time that I went out with Frank, it was the middle of winter. We went up to Wisconsin to work on an engine. Everywhere I looked was snow and gray skies. Bleak, I'd call it, and cold. My feet were cold, my hands were cold, and my lips were blue. It didn't help that we were working on a cold dead engine with cold steel tools. You couldn't always wear gloves. Sometimes when you are working on an engine you have to be able to feel the parts. So, off go the gloves and then a bolt or nut might stick to your fingers if you weren't careful. Anyway, it was cold and snowy. After we cranked that engine over, we packed up and headed home.

I took my turn driving on the way home. I started driving at the age of 11. The snow was blowing sideways and the roads were icy.

"Faster, Billy!" Frank encouraged. I put my foot down on the pedal and faster we went, but not fast enough for Frank. "Faster, Billy, faster," he yelled with a smile on his face. I pressed the accelerator down farther. "Come on, Billy, faster," and Frank reached his foot over and pressed it on mine and yelled, "That's it, Billy, let's go!"

I really felt that Frank trusted me. He put me in a situation that could have gotten us both killed, but he trusted my abilities. He knew I would remain calm and not panic, even as he pressed me.

In addition to helping Frank, I always found some work to do. I did odd jobs for neighbors. I was good with my hands and could fix things. I also sold papers. Three cents a copy—and when big news broke, I'd sell an 'Extra' for a little more.

I rode my bike out to the golf course and got a job as a caddy. I thought that if I got on there, I might get some good tip money. Boy, was I wrong. The richer the man, the smaller the tip. Sometimes the fella would send me off to do something at the eighteenth hole. When I'd come back, he'd be gone—no tip at all.

Another thing a no-tipper would do was to get involved in a long conversation until the caddy could wait no longer. It would be rude to interrupt, and if you did, the guy would act offended.

"So, boy, you think a doctor like me would try to stiff a hard-working young man?"

"Hell, yes, you would," I would think to myself.

The long conversation type was a really skilled non-tipper. Under no circumstance could he let the conversation die until the caddy gave up and walked away. Fortunately, I also caddied for some good people who *were* good tippers and treated me right. As a result of my caddying days I grew to dislike the game. Golf would *never* be one of my hobbies.

When I was 13, I got hit by a car. It was my fault. I was riding like a bat out of hell and rode right into him, which left me laid out on the street. That was the only time I was ever knocked cold. I felt like I was dreaming. I could hear voices through the fog in my head.

"Is he dead?" I heard someone say.

"I don't know!"

"Give him some air!"

"He came out of nowhere!"

I blinked and opened my eyes. Looking around, I could see a crowd of people. I touched my head and looked at the dark blood on my fingers. I sank back and closed my eyes for a bit. When I re-opened them, I saw the policeman standing there, "Don't move, son."

"I'm okay," I said as I got up to my elbows and then to a seated position. I looked at my bike; it was a wreck. Then, seeing I was not dead, the man I'd hit started complaining about the dent in his fender, which was about the size of my head. The police officer looked at him and told him to hit the road.

"You're lucky this boy is alive," the officer growled. "If he didn't have such a hard head, I might be charging you with manslaughter." The policeman looked at me and said, "With a head like that you must be Irish." I smiled weakly. "We better get you to a hospital."

I slowly stood up and told him Doc Bradley could check me out. The officer picked up my bike and said, "All right, then I'll go with you."

We walked together to the doc's. I thanked him and told him where I lived. He said he'd tell Mom where I was and what happened. He carried my bike to the house and told Ma the whole story.

Doc Bradley looked me over real good, sewed me up, and walked me home. "He'll live, Thelma, but keep him quiet for a few days and I'll check on him later."

I'll never forget the time I got sick real bad. I was so sick that all I could do was lie in my bed for a week. I had a high fever, sweats, and chills. Every inch of my body ached, and Ma thought I was going to die. Doc Bradley said the only thing that could be done was to keep me quiet and give me as much water as I could take. I drank the water and in my fevered state I thought about an old friend of mine.

Joey, me, and some other boys were out playing one blistering summer day. We were hot and sweaty and tired after a long day of playing. I said so long to Joey and he went into his kitchen, opened the fridge, and pulled out a pitcher of ice water. He drank and drank that ice-cold water. Then he dropped dead. After that, I never drank water out of the refrigerator.

While I was sick Ma stayed with me day and night. She kept my sheets and cold compresses changed, and she kept Richard away from me. I think she sent him to Grandma Kasper's. After a week, my fever broke and I made my recovery. I don't know why or how I got sick. I figured it was germs or a virus, but, hell, I didn't know. After a couple weeks I had my strength back and was back to normal. But from that day on, whenever I washed dishes I got the water scalding hot and would pour bleach in the water. The dishes would smell of bleach. Richard complained about the smell of the glasses when he drank his milk.

One day, I went down the street to a little store in Harvey. The store was owned by a tall, thin old man who spoke with a Polish accent. The store had wooden floors, a short counter with a register on it, and shelves of canned goods and other items. It was kind of a small convenience store that had a little bit of everything. Right next to the front window stood a pinball machine. The old man was smart; a lot of kids would come in and spend their money on that machine. I was one of them.

On that particular day, Tony was playing the pinball machine. Tony was a couple inches taller than me, but I think I outweighed him (I never starved). He was sixteen and attended Thornton Township High School. I was thirteen years old. Well, anyway, he was there first and it was his to play.

I wandered around the store, talked to the old man, and looked at some of the stuff on the shelves. Tony kept playing. He would finish a game and give me a dirty look. I tried to ignore his looks, and waited patiently for my turn. I waited and I waited and I waited. Finally, I thought he was done. He exclaimed "Darn it," and stood there looking at the machine.

I said, "Okay, it's my turn now."

He slowly turned his head toward me and said, "You can play when I *say* you can play."

Now, I never started a fight—that's one of the rules, you know—but I had had about enough. "It's my turn. I waited all day for you, now let me have a turn."

He turned to me and said, "I'll let you have it, fatty!" It was on. He lunged for me, but I was a lot faster and stronger than Tony had judged. I side-stepped him and got two good shots in as he tripped past me. Then it was all fists and elbows flying. The old man yelled, "Stop it, boys!"

As we wrestled around, the store owner was desperately reaching and grabbing for items that were falling from the shelves. We were really rocking the place. If I hadn't been so busy, I think I would have laughed at that old man running around his store yelling, "Stop it, stop it!" as he tried to save his merchandise. I got the better of Tony and knocked him down with a good hard combination. He was bleeding from his nose and mouth. I was okay, but I was breathing kind of hard.

Just then, the bell on the door rang and in walked Ed Beinor. Ed was about six years older than me. In Harvey we called him "Beefy" because he was over six foot two and weighed 210 or 220 pounds. He lived right down the street from me, and was home on break from school at Notre Dame, where he played football. (Later on, he even played pro ball for the Washington Redskins.) He had watched the fight through the window. Ed looked at me, then at Tony, and then back at me.

"That was a pretty good fight. You are pretty tough for a little chubby kid. Fast with his fists, isn't he, Tony?" Tony nodded. Then, Ed instructed, "Stand up and shake his hand, Tony, cause you two just had a real good fight. Guys who have a good fight need to appreciate the thing and respect a worthy opponent, just like on the football field." Beinor looked at me and said, "Maybe we will square off someday on the football field. Better yet, I think I'd rather you were on my team." He laughed and slapped Tony and me on the back as we shook hands. "Come on now, guys, let's help the old man pick up the place."

29

As we picked up, I thought to myself, "We will never play football together, Ed. My mother thinks football is too dangerous."

I had asked Ma on more than one occasion to let me play football. She would just say, "No, you'll break your neck. I've read about those boys getting killed or crippled. You may not play football."

So, that was that. No football for me.

When I was growing up in Harvey, we always rented. We lived in three different houses over the years. Wood-framed houses with a coal furnace. Nothing fancy. We would have to move whenever the landlord said. They might suddenly sell the house, and we would have to pack up and move. Or some relative of the owner might need a place to live and we would get the boot.

Billy D.'s mother, Thelma,
at the House in Harvey they lost

It was in 1937 when Frank and Mom bought their first home. It was a nice-looking, bungalow-style house with stucco walls. Best of all, it had steam heat. The house was cooler in the summer than any house we had lived in...and warmer in the winter. The furnace was still coal fired.

With steam heat you have a boiler filled with water. The fuel—in our case, coal—is fired and heats up the water, which turns into steam. The steam travels through pipes and into the rooms of the house via radiators. The radiator consists of a unit that stands three or four feet tall and maybe three or four feet wide. The steam travels into the radiator's pipes, which go up and down in loops several times. This up, down, and turning exposes surface area of the un-insulated pipes. This, in turn, produces radiant heat that warms the room. Ah, yes, a warm room, relatively speaking.

It didn't seem like we were in that house very long when Buda cut Frank's wages by 75 dollars a month. We stayed a couple months after that, but in the end, we lost the house. After that, in Frank's mind he was finished with Buda. He was a good engine man, and had done everything they asked. He traveled and installed and repaired their engines. He knew he could do better. He didn't quit right away, but after they cut his pay, he kept his ears open for another opportunity.

In 1938, I attended Thornton Township High School. As a high school student, I took college preparatory classes, like algebra, geometry, and so forth. I took shop for one year, but decided that saws were not my game. I had two different teachers that year...neither was very encouraging. My first teacher had two fingers missing. When I saw this, I clenched my teeth and looked at my hand and thought, "Oooh." The second instructor walked into class and didn't have any fingers on his left hand. Only the thumb remained. That was it for me. I very carefully cut the wood for my project—bookends, I think. After that, no more shop for Bill.

In 1938, Frank and I tuned in the radio and heard Joe Louis beat Max Schmeling for the heavyweight boxing championship. We both enjoyed a good fight. At other times, we listened to car races (like the Indy 500), baseball, and football games.

That year, minimum wage was 40 cents per hour and unemployment was 19 percent. We were fortunate that Frank had a skill that was in demand. He was never out of work.

Also in 1938, the paper carried the story of a hurricane that hit the East Coast. A 40-foot wave crashed into Long Island. Sixty-three-thousand people were left homeless; 700 people died. There were a lot of questions and finger pointing. The National Weather Service gave little warning of the approaching danger.

This was also the year that the British Prime Minister, Neville Chamberlain, agreed to allow Hitler to occupy Czechoslovakia. Chamberlain declared, "Peace in our time." Meanwhile, the Germans were building a powerful military that threatened world peace. One year earlier, Japan had begun its aggression against China.

On New Year's Eve in 1938, Billy Sièmers, Charles Armington, Louis Stubs, Harvey Goodwine, and I got together at Harvey's parents' house. The Goodwines, the proud owners of a nice collection of wine, had gone to a New Year's Eve party. We helped ourselves. We thought that they had so many bottles they would never miss a couple or three bottles. That was the first time I got drunk.

After we drank the wine we went to a theater and watched a movie. We talked out loud in the theater and enjoyed the movie more than anyone else. Those guys were good friends and I liked cutting loose with them. I couldn't tell you the title of the movie or the name of the theater. All I remember was we had a good time and I somehow found my way home. Mom and Dad never found out.

The next morning, Ma got me up early. Stomach turning, I made my way to the kitchen table. My head was spinning. I sat down to a plate of the runniest eggs I'd ever seen. I excused myself and headed back to my room.

In September of 1939, Britain and France declared war on Germany after the Nazis invaded Poland. Back then, newspapers would print an 'Extra,' an unscheduled newspaper edition that covered a special or big event. My brother Richard was a cute little six year old. I got him dressed and said, "Come on, Richie, we are gonna sell some newspapers."

I picked up as many Extras announcing the start of the war as I could. Then, I staked out a busy street corner and put Richie on the curb. He was a little guy and I didn't want him to get run over. I also knew that cute sold papers. I stood out in traffic and sold in between the cars. Richie stood on the curb, smiled real big, and sold the hell out of those papers. A regular paper sold for three cents. I sold these papers at 50 cents a copy. It was supply and demand. People wanted to read about the war. They paid the price and I sold out. Richie was going to need a bigger piggy bank.

In 1939, Richie started school. He attended the same elementary school that I had attended. His teacher was also Miss Way. Rich was held back and had to repeat first grade. One thing I didn't mention about Miss Way—she was mom's cousin.

In 1940, Frank finally left Buda. He had worked for them for as long as I could remember. But between being on the road and losing our house, he had a bad taste in his mouth. He took a job with an engine company in Chicago. I left Thornton Township High School and Harvey, Illinois, never to return. We lived in Chicago for three months. Frank did not like the new company. Some men, headhunters, knew Frank was talented and told him about a company that needed a good engine man, and that they were willing to make it worth his while. The job was with National Supply Company, which built engines and compressors. The engines could power generators, or they could be connected to a compressor to push oil or gas through pipelines.

Unfortunately, National Supply was located in Philadelphia.

Becoming A Man

Philadelphia, Pennsylvania

The company wanted Frank immediately; he accepted the offer and headed to the City of Brotherly Love. I will never forget the Saturday in October 1940 when Grandma Kasper came to our house to visit. She had been at the house for about an hour and saw that the 1935 Chevy was parked outside. She wandered into a few rooms and then came back to the kitchen for her coffee.

"Where is Frank?" she asked.

There was a long silence and Ma's jaw dropped. Finally, she said in a high voice, "Didn't he tell you?"

"Tell me what?" Marguerite responded.

"We are moving to Philadelphia; Frank is already there working."

Grandma was beside herself. She paced around saying, "I can't believe it. He is where?"

I don't know why Frank didn't tell her. I never asked. If I had asked, he might have said that he hates to say goodbye or that his mom had Dick, Wayne, and Henrietta; therefore, his absence was not important...or some horse shit like that. But I didn't ask, so I don't know the answer to that question. What I do know is that the next few weeks were a very busy time for us. National Supply was not going to pay to move a new hire who might not work out, so we put all of our furniture and appliances up for sale. A yard sale. We sold almost everything but the clothes on our backs. We said goodbye to our family and friends, and Doc Bradley lost a very good customer.

We packed that 1935 Chevy with all the clothes and belongings we could carry. With Frank in Philadelphia, I was the man of the house and it was my job to drive the family to our new home. I loaded Mom, Grandma Bailey, Rich, and Fritz the dog into that Chevy. We must have been quite a sight as we drove down the road with Chicago and Harvey in our rear view.

The Chevy used a quart of oil every hundred miles. We drove about 260 miles that first day, and stayed at a tourist home that night. Common in the 1940s, tourist homes were located along the most traveled roads. There were not hotels and lodges along state routes at that time. A tourist home usually had five or so rooms for guests. The only advertising was a sign in front of the house that said, "Tourist Home." I would drive as long as I could, but I had to make sure that I didn't travel too far and too late. I didn't want to miss a place to stay and force us to sleep along the side of the road. I was in charge. I was responsible.

On the second day of our trip we stopped at a little diner for lunch. Afterward, we headed back to the Chevy and it would not start. I knew it was the generator (alternator). I had Grandma and Rich get out of the car.

"Ma, you get behind the wheel and I'll push. When we get some speed up, I'll holler and you pop the clutch to start the car."

Richie yelled, "Let me help you push, Billy."

I looked down at him and said, "Okay, Rich, but you do as I say."

So, Richie and I pushed and pushed until we got up enough speed. Then, I yelled, "Now, Ma!" Thelma let out the clutch and the engine came to life. I blocked the wheel, we loaded into the car, and off we went. Now, every hundred miles I added a quart of oil *and* we had to make sure we parked on a hill so I could get the car to coast and then pop the clutch to get it started.

As we traveled across Ohio, we came up behind a car in Toledo. The car stopped short and I hit him. I got out of the car and he tried to push me around, but I had none of that.

"You stopped short on purpose. You caused this to collect money from us out-of-townees, you son-of-a-bitch." That stopped him in his tracks.

He stammered and sputtered and finally said, "No matter what you say, you still hit me, and the police will side with me." I told that SOB to call the police.

Ma got out of the car and looked at him sternly. "What do you want?" she asked in a low voice.

"Fifty dollars," the gangster replied.

"I'll give you twenty." She pulled a twenty out and ordered him to get. We headed on down the road.

It took me three days to drive the family to Philadelphia. I followed the river to our new home, which was a row house. Some people called them "shotgun houses." A shotgun house is about 12 feet wide. Our house had a front door with a window beside it, and five rooms in a row with no hallways. They called it a shotgun house because you could shoot a shotgun in the front door and the pellets would exit the back door without hitting a wall. Anyway, we were home.

The next day I took Ma into town and she bought new furniture and appliances. Frank was making a good living working for National Supply. We had extra spending money for the first time.

Winter came and went. It was the spring of 1941. Now, row houses, or shotgun houses, all pretty much look alike. One Friday evening I was listening to the radio. Frank and Ma and Grandma were reading and Richard was playing on the floor with Fritz. The front door opened and in walked our neighbor, Bob. We all looked up, stunned that someone had just entered our house unannounced. He walked into the house a few feet and then swayed to a stop. It was obvious that Bob had really tied one on...he just stood there with a confused look on his face. He wiped his mouth and burped a little. We just sat there and looked at Bob. Fritz didn't even bark. I think he was as stunned as we were.

Bob looked around and an incredulous look came over his face. "June," he called. "June, come out here. There are people in our house."

Thelma looked at him and shook her head. "Robert, you are drunk out of your head. June isn't in the next room, she is next door at your house, where you should be. Billy, help Mr. Anderson over to his house."

I jumped up. "Come on, Mr. Anderson. I'll get you home." I reached out to him and he took my hand like a small child would.

Recognizing me, he said, "Okay, Billy. You are a good kid." I walked Mr. Anderson over to his house and his wife, June.

Mr. Anderson was a happy kind of drunk. That is, he wasn't mean. Bob would work all week and be as normal as anyone, but on Friday he would get paid, cash his check, and head to the saloon. He visited our house the next Friday and the next. It seemed as though he was a regular part of our Friday routine. If he didn't show up, one of us would check on him the next day to make sure Bob was all right.

Ma would say to Frank, "I don't know why June puts up with that shit!"

Frank would reply, "I don't know, but he doesn't hurt anyone and besides, that's not our business."

Frank, Bill and Raymond in Philadelphia

Richie and I had nine-and-a-half years between us, but he was getting old enough that we could do some things together. I would take him with me when I'd go to the store or on an errand for Ma. Sometimes on Saturdays, I would take Rich to a movie.

In the spring of 1941, Frank and I bought a couple motorcycles. We had fun riding them around. Raymond brought Shirley May to visit, and I let Raymond ride my bike with Frank. We had a ball with those bikes. We had as much fun working on the bikes as we did riding them.

One Saturday while Raymond and Shirley May were visiting, we went to Pennypack Park. It covered 1,600 acres and had woodlands, meadows, wetlands, and Pennypack Creek, which emptied into the Delaware River. Pennypack Park had places to play, trails, and an old stone bridge that was built in 1697. There were also many other historic sites and buildings—none of which interested Richie.

We hiked around and eventually found our way to the creek. I never really cared for water. I couldn't swim, and didn't want to learn. Richie went down to the water's edge to look for some fish and crawdads. He spotted some fish and tried to walk out on some rocks to investigate. He slipped on a rock and I heard the yell and splash. It had rained for a couple of days, so the creek was up and running fast.

Grandma Bailey stood up and yelled, "Richard is drowning!" We all jumped up and ran as fast as we could. By the time we got to Rich, a man had pulled him out of the water and onto the shore. Rich was spitting and sputtering, but he was alive. We thanked the man. He said that he was just glad he was there. Richie was wet and cold and ready to go, so we packed up our picnic and headed home.

Ma really liked living in Philly...that city had a lot going on. It had shipyards that built ships for the U.S. Navy. While we were there, the U.S.S. New Jersey was being built. The Battleship New Jersey would become America's most decorated battleship. Of course, Philly was also rich with history. Elfreth's Alley is the oldest continuously inhabited street in America. The Continental Congress met in Philadelphia, and the Liberty Bell is on display there.

Yes, Ma liked Philly, but I think she really liked that it was an easy drive to New York City, the most populated city in the United States. New York City had the tallest buildings and the busiest harbor in America. If a person didn't want to drive in the city, there were taxis everywhere and a subway system that carried riders to every corner of the city. And the sites—the Empire State Building, the Statue of Liberty, theaters, museums, Central Park, and more. We drove to New York City a dozen times in 1941. I did enjoy our family drives to the city.

Summer came and went, and I was back in school for my senior year. Frank came home from work in late September and said, "Pack up, Mom, we're moving again."

Ma asked, "What happened? Did you lose your job?"

"They are closing down and moving the whole operation to Springfield, Ohio."

"Springfield, Ohio! Where in the world is that?"

"It's between Dayton and Columbus. It sits right on Route 40. It's a small town, but it has a lot of industry and a good workforce. But the best news is that this time the company is moving us!"

Defining Moments

Springfield, Ohio

So, in November of 1941 we said goodbye to Philadelphia. Grandma Bailey, Frank, Ma, Rich, me, and Fritz loaded into the car and off we went. Our furniture made the trip in a moving truck. We stayed overnight in a tourist home along the way. We arrived in Springfield, Ohio, and stayed in a tourist home that first night. Frank asked the owner of the home if he knew of a place that we could rent. The man said that his cousin had a home on Southern Avenue for rent. The address was 316 West Southern. He arranged for us to see the house the next day. We walked through the house and talked terms. Later that day, we were moving in.

That week, I enrolled at Springfield High School, and Ma took Richie for his first day of school in a new city. Springfield High was my fourth high school in four years.

I was downtown after school one day, a couple days before Thanksgiving. A man was standing on the street corner selling geese, which were very much alive, for Thanksgiving dinner. I had some money in my pocket and I thought, "What the hell, this might be good." Boy, was I wrong. I tucked that honking, squirming bird under my arm and headed home.

Mom and Grandma looked at the bird and said, "What are we supposed to do with that?"

I told them, "It's Thanksgiving dinner."

Richie thought it was great, though he wanted it to be his pet. I told Mom that the man gave me instructions on how to clean and cook it. She agreed to help me, and the next day we got to work.

The evening before Thanksgiving we put the goose on a water-only diet. Thanksgiving morning, I grabbed the bird and tied a rope around his feet and looped the other end over a tree branch. Boy, did that bird buck and squirm. As it hung there, I grabbed it and held it still—well, as still as I could. Mom came at it with a knife. We looked at each other and gritted our teeth. With me holding on for dear life, Ma took a cut at it. The cut wasn't deep and missed the jugular. Now I was *really* in for a ride. I held onto that bird with all my might while Ma took another cut...a good, deep cut into the jugular. It was not a pretty sight. We plucked the goose and gutted it. I can tell you that after that experience, we never again purchased a live animal for a meal. I never again looked at a goose the same way.

A couple weeks later, I took Richard to the State Theater in downtown Springfield. We were watching a movie, when the flick suddenly stopped and the lights went up. The theater manager walked up on stage with a paper in his hand and read, "The Japanese have attacked Pearl Harbor." I wasn't surprised that we were at war. I was, however, shocked at how we were brought into the war.

The next day, men and boys began lining up at the recruiter stations. In Chicago, Uncle Raymond joined. He was too old to be in the regular infantry, so they assigned him to work in a field hospital.

I tried to focus on finishing high school. I always had to work to get good grades. Things didn't always come easy to me, but I studied hard and got good grades. All of my classes were college preparatory.

I sat down with Frank and told him that I just wasn't sure what I wanted to do. I told him that I wanted to fly, but I knew I couldn't pass the physical. I didn't have two left feet or anything like that. I was pretty good at sports, but not a star athlete like Ed Beinor. Frank told me that there was plenty of time. "Don't rush into a decision Billy. Don't count yourself out. There are a lot of planes doing a lot of different jobs."

I graduated from Springfield High School in May 1942. Frank got me a job at National Supply, which put me to work as an engine tester. I had field experience and knew engines, so I didn't start as a general laborer or sweeping the floors.

The factory was a low-profile brick and concrete building that snaked along Sheridan Avenue in Springfield. This plant manufactured the large diesels from molten iron to finished engine or compressor field ready. The foundry was a hot, dusty, smoke-filled place. The men working there had dirty black faces from working around the sand and iron. They would get in the shower and try to cough up and blow the sand out of their sinuses and lungs.

It was in the foundry that wood patterns were used to make the sand cores and molds. Sand mixed with chemicals held the patterned shape. The cores were placed in the molds and the mold was sealed. The sand mold was made inside a steel flask. The flask held the sand in place. The cope is the top

Billy D. graduate of Springfield High School, June 1943

half of the mold, and the drag is the bottom half of the mold. The top and bottom were held together by cope seal and large clamps. Large cranes that spanned the width of the foundry carried the ladles filled with liquid iron. Iron was poured into risers (holes) in the cope; smoke and the burnt-sand smell filled the air. After the iron cooled and hardened, the flasks (or molds) were opened. Red-hot sand poured out, revealing the rough product. The remainder of the sand was knocked out of the casting and metal fins were removed. Shot blast was next. The shot blast operator smoothed the casting by directing a high pressure blast of sand at the iron.

Once the casting was smooth and clean, it moved to the last stop in the foundry. Chip and grinders prepared the casting for the shop. Pneumatic hand tools ground and chipped away at rough spots and unneeded iron. The casting was transported to the machine shop.

Oil and stones were used in the process of machining. I always liked the smell that the oil combined with the friction of the presses and drilling machines made. Machining completed, holes bored, and threads created, the castings moved to the assembly floor. Once all the pieces of the engine reached the floor, they were assembled. The giant engine took shape, and when finished, was placed on the test stand. The engine was adjusted and tuned. It was run for several test hours and then was ready for shipment. The engines were behemoths. Some engine blocks alone could be 25 feet long. A man would need an eight-foot stepladder to see the top of an engine.

On August 7, 1942, I turned 19 years old. When a person is trying to make a decision, everyone has something to say about it. I got a lot of suggestions. "Sign up and take your chances." "You don't want to be a pilot. Join the Navy."

I heard that reconnaissance pilots did not have to pass as rigorous mental and physical tests as the regular Army Air Corps pilots, so one Saturday I drove over to Dayton to see about flying reconnaissance. I found my way to the correct building and office, grabbed a clipboard, and filled out the questionnaire. The duty sergeant read over my application and called me to his desk.

"Have you been turned down by the Army Air Corps?"

"No, sir, I haven't. I don't think I could pass the physical."

"You have to be turned down before we can consider you. So, get yourself over to Patterson Field and take the test."

I thanked him and told him that I would be back soon. Unfortunately, I had wasted most of the day and there wasn't time to go to Patterson. I decided I would take the test the following Saturday.

Patterson Field was a sprawling air base in Dayton, Ohio. It was an Air Corps supply depot, testing base, and the largest air base in the United States. I had to make an appointment for my test. I was directed to the proper gate and then to the building where I would take the test.

Once again, I filled out the information sheet on the clipboard. There were two fellas ahead of me. I think they came together. The sergeant read over my application and in a loud voice in front of those two men said,

"Son, you'd be wasting your time taking this test." He pointed to the two men. "These boys here have finished their sophomore year at Ohio State. Why don't you just go on home?" He wasn't asking me to go; he was telling me.

I sure didn't like his way or his loud mouth. I replied, "I think I'll just stay and give it a try, Sergeant." He gave me a dirty look. I don't know why he had to be that way. It was no skin off his nose if I passed or failed the test. So, he handed the sophomores the test, and slapped mine down on my desk. "Begin," he ordered.

When I get mad, I get stubborn. I get determined. That sergeant sure pushed my buttons. "The hell with reconnaissance," I thought. I wanted to be an Army Air Corps pilot.

I don't remember how long it took me to finish the test, but I answered every question. The sergeant called time, collected the papers, and handed them to the grader. Then we all sat there, wondering and waiting. The Ohio State boys laughed and talked between themselves. I sat there quietly.

The sergeant was handed the results and read them aloud. "Sophomore number one—" he looked up, "failed. Sophomore number two—" he scowled, "failed." Their jaws dropped. Now that sergeant looked really mad. "Kasper—passed." His face flushed. So did mine, except for a different reason. "Sophomores from the Ohio State University, you are dismissed. Kasper, take this paper down the hall for your physical. I know you won't pass that. It would take a gallon of grease and a shoe horn to get you behind the stick of an airplane."

He was right. I was five foot nine and one-half inches. I weighed around 200 pounds. But I passed the test...I passed the damned thing! I could do it. Bring on the next hurdle. I was going to do it. The doctors and technicians administered a battery of tests. My eyesight was 20-20 in the left eye and 20-10 in the right. Excellent peripheral vision. Good eyes for spotting enemy aircraft. My reflexes were excellent, breathing great, mental great. I passed all of the tests. Afterward, a doctor came up to me and sat down. "You did very well on all our tests, but you have to get your weight down. You have 30 days to get your weight to 183 pounds. If you don't, you will not qualify for pilot training. Can you do that, son?"

"You bet I can," I replied.

For the next 30 days I followed a strict diet...I starved myself. I would get up early before work and run. My boss at work gave me calisthenics to do on my breaks. If I was working out, I wasn't eating. After 30 days I went back to Patterson Field for my weigh-in. I weighed 181 pounds. I did it! "What now?" I asked.

"Go home and we will contact you when we need you."

"Go home?" I thought. So, that's what I did. It was October of 1942. I went home and went back to work. The hard work was far from over. I knew that. I kept myself in shape and checked out aviation books from the library. I studied mathematics and physics.

PILOT TRAINING

THE JOURNEY BEGINS

The call came in April of 1943. I was ordered to Fort Hayes in Columbus, Ohio, and was directed to a briefing room. There were about 30 of us, and an officer came in and told us to have a seat. He looked us over and said, "This looks to be about the right size group. They want about 30 men in Nashville for Classification that is preflight, so I'm sending this group. That means no Basic Training in Texas for you."

Every man in the room was all smiles at the thought of skipping Basic and going to Classification. We would be able to get into the fight before the war was over. "The sergeant will give you all of the details. Carry on." The officer gathered up his papers and left the room.

The sergeant surveyed us and let out a "Humph, so you men are all pretty pleased about skipping Basic. Think you are pretty special? Get that thought out of your thick skulls. The only reason you are leap-frogging to Classification is the Nazis are killing pilots so fast we can't fill the planes."

"What a kill-joy," I thought. The smiles disappeared from the men's faces and the room got real quiet.

"Now, if you make it through Classification and don't kill yourself learning to fly, the Germans will probably shoot your ass off. Or maybe you'll get lucky and wash out as a pilot and they'll stick you in a B17 as a belly gunner. Then you'll just get your dick shot off. Congratulations, men."

So, they loaded us up and shipped us to Nashville, Tennessee, to the Army Air Forces Classification Center, the induction station for new cadets. We learned how to make our beds (bounce a quarter off the bed) and eat square meals, eyes always facing forward. You might wonder what I mean when I say they taught us to eat a square meal. They taught us that a cadet picked up his tray and walked—back straight, eyes forward—to his seat. Once seated, at attention, the cadet scooped or forked his food, raising the eating utensil parallel to the cadet's body. The utensil, with food on it, was raised to mouth height and then traveled a straight line into the cadet's mouth. The utensil was removed from the mouth and followed the path in reverse back to the plate. The cadet did not look up, down, or side to side while eating. The cadet's posture and eating utensil movement created an imaginary square.

We were given several physical examinations and we took aptitude tests. We ran everywhere. No walking allowed. They really worked us. I thought they wanted to kill us. Based on the tests and physical training, we were classified. The Air Corps used the test results to determine our skills and talent, and then it was on for more training. We would move into pilot, bombardier, navigator, or gunner training.

I moved on to pilot training. Next stop: Maxwell Field in Montgomery, Alabama, for Preflight. In 1910, the Wright Brothers opened one of the world's first flying schools at what would become Maxwell Field. We didn't fly here; this was preflight training. We studied the mechanics and physics of flight. I worked hard. I was not going to wash out. I went to town only once in two months. The rest of the time I spent studying. We had to pass math and science courses, then once we knew the theory, we applied our knowledge to meteorology, aeronautics, deflection shooting, and three-dimensional thinking.

Meteorology is the scientific study of the atmosphere. We learned about clouds, their movement, and types—cirrus, nimbostratus, and alto-cumulus. Cloud coverage is broken down into tenths:

$0/_{10}$	clear/sunny
$1/_{10}$	fair (high wispy cirrus)
$2/_{10}$ – $3/_{10}$	mostly sunny
$4/_{10}$ – $6/_{10}$	partly cloudy
$7/_{10}$ – $8/_{10}$	mostly cloudy
$9/_{10}$	broken clouds
$10/_{10}$	overcast/cloudy

If I didn't make it as a pilot I could be a weatherman.

Aeronautics is the study of the motion of air and how it interacts with objects. We learned about drag, slipstreams, lift, and more.

Deflection shooting is a technique used when firing at a moving target. The cadet is taught how to lead the moving target, taking into account the speed of both aircraft and distance to the target. We learned that other factors influenced the flight of a projectile. Cross-winds altered the flight of a shell. The thin air at high altitude made a projectile fly faster. Temperatures can also affect the flight of a shell.

We used the link-trainer. There were five of these at Maxwell. The trainer was a box with wings. The student sat inside of it and practiced operating a simulated aircraft in flight. A technician monitored the student. When we climbed in the Link we knew we were getting close to the real thing.

Link Trainer

The High Altitude Chamber was located conveniently at the back of sick bay. The chamber looked like a half-submerged submarine, and it smelled something like sick bay with all of its cleaning and other odors. We would enter the chamber through a steel door. There were round porthole windows at either end of the chamber. We would sit in two rows facing each other, and the instructor would say, "Okay, we are going to climb to 5,000 feet." We would yawn to pop our ears, and put on oxygen masks. I forget how high we went—probably over 20,000 feet. We were required to do math and write legibly while in the chamber. Men washed out because they couldn't cope with the stresses of high altitude simulation.

We practiced firing hand guns. We had to be proficient at shooting or we would be washed out. A downed pilot's only defense was a handgun. We learned how to pack a parachute. I knew that I didn't want to use one, but I was sure going to learn to pack one right.

We continued our physical training, square meals, tight beds, and other disciplines. We were subjected to tear gas. We were gassed and had to perform mental and physical activities while wearing our mask. On top of all that, there was hazing dished out by the upperclassmen. They might harass a cadet by repeatedly making him remake his bed, double timing his running and exercise, and just plain being nasty to a fella.

There was one upperclassman...I'll call him Aspane. Aspane really got into his hazing, and I was his project. I think he enjoyed himself too much. I remember one time Aspane came up to me while I was in formation and yelled, "Give me an inch of that belt, cadet." I had to suck in and pull that belt tight and cut off an inch of the belt and give it to him.

When I was an upperclassman, I never gave a guy the kind of shit that Aspane gave me. I thought, "When we both get commissioned and are of equal rank, I am going to put lumps all over you!"

Primary Flying School was at Camden Army Air Field in Arkansas. It was here that I soloed. A cadet had to solo at or before eight recorded hours. The Air Corps had goals with time tables. If you didn't meet a goal in the prescribed time, you washed out. I wasn't about to wash out.

In Camden, we trained in the Stearman biplane, a two-winged plane. It had fixed landing gear, which means the wheels could not be raised or lowered. The trainer had two open-air cockpits—pilot and trainer. The engine would whistle and sputter when first cranked. It was the type of whistle you make by blowing through your bottom teeth, lips slightly apart. Then it would rumble to life. The pilot controlled the plane with a stick, no steering wheel. Throttle and aileron controls. The throttle increased or decreased the speed of the aircraft. The stick controlled the rudder and flaps. The rudder turned the plane left and right. Flaps (on the rear stabilizer) enabled the aircraft to gain or decrease altitude. Pedals at the pilot's feet controlled the ailerons, which tilted the plane. One wing raised and the other simultaneously lowered.

One Friday night, two cadets went to a roadhouse on the outskirts of Camden. They ordered a couple of drinks. One of the boys started talking to a local girl, and she was talking back in a flirtatious way. The bartender signaled the bouncer at the door. The cadet stood up and walked to the door, but the bouncer barred the door so no one could come or go. The bartender reached under the bar, grabbed a club, and hit the other cadet. The bouncer hit the cadet nearest the door with a club. He crumpled over and some men jumped on him and began kicking and hitting him. The cadet at the bar was staggered. One man grabbed his arms, while another hit him repeatedly. They were dumped on the side of the road near the base's main gate. Those boys spent a week in the hospital.

We had some men who had been in the Army before the war. One of them was Sergeant Kalinowsky. Kalinowsky was a tough bird. Before he enlisted, he was a coal miner. He gathered a group of us together. "Boys, we are not gonna put up with this shit. I am not having any of this. A man has a right to have a drink and talk to a pretty girl if he wants."

The next Friday, we all loaded up and headed to the outskirts of Camden. We were in pretty damned good shape, and we were ready for a fight. Two by two, we went into the roadhouse. We spread out once inside. Kalinowsky directed one cadet to stand near the door and the bouncer. Kalinowsky called to the bartender and ordered a drink. The bartender set the drink on the bar, and Kalinowsky whispered something in his ear. He got an angry look on his face, signaled the bouncer, and reached for the club. Kalinowsky caught him by the shirt and threw a right cross. POW! His eyes rolled up and he was out.

The bouncer stepped toward the scene at the bar. The cadet at the door swung him around. The bouncer swung hard and high. The cadet was ready; he ducked the punch and swung hard into the bouncer's belly. The bouncer lost his dinner on the spot. It was on.

Victor A. Guebard, John J. Dennin, Alan C. Judd, George E. Kalinowsky, Arthur G. Kozacka, and instructor H. O. Dabney

Kalinowsky told the boys, "Now, when it starts, come in one at a time. We will take them one-on-one. No two-on-one." We cleaned house that night. When a local tried to jump in, he was smacked down hard by a waiting cadet. When the bartender and his bouncer came to, they were told that cadets would come into his place and they would *not* be ganged up on. We looked at all the men in that roadhouse. We looked them in the eye to make sure they got the message. From that time on, we ran that place. We didn't hurt anyone, but everyone knew that we would take care of our own. We just wanted to have a little fun without getting our heads busted.

About 300 miles down the road from Camden was our next stop—Walnut Ridge, Arkansas. In Walnut Ridge, I trained in the AT-6, The Texan. I liked flying the Stearman better than the AT-6. The Stearman was fun to fly. The AT-6 was one step away from combat aircraft. It had a single fixed wing, and produced 550 horsepower. There was plenty of room in the cockpit for an instructor. The aircraft resembled a Japanese Zero. This was also the first plane I flew that had retractable landing gear. We learned how to land in crosswinds, on short runways, and we learned how to handle stalls.

Clifford H. Vaughn, Alan Kriegbaum, Billy D. Kasper, Henry A. Bennett, Robert J. Haley, and instructor Leon G. Cobb

I only went to town one time while I was at Walnut Ridge. Men continued to wash out for one reason or another. Before I entered flight training, I thought that people who had private pilot licenses had an advantage. Boy, was I wrong. The military demanded the cadet fly the plane the military way. The boys who had private licenses, in many cases, had bad habits. If those cadets did not quickly learn new habits, they were washed out. Many of them did wash out.

At Walnut Ridge, I logged 77 flying hours, but some of the most important hours I spent were on the ground. There were days that we couldn't fly. The weather would keep us grounded. It was on these days that my instructor, Leon Cobb, would gather all of his students together and talk. He talked about situations that may come up. He discussed how to handle stalls, balloon landings, and more. He answered our questions. He made us think. I know that he saved my life. I owe him my life.

Other cadets were not as fortunate as me. At one point, we lost five men in five days. They just spun in. I guess they stalled their plane and couldn't recover. I don't really know why they crashed. Flying was a dangerous business. These incidents brought that reality home.

It was also at Walnut Ridge that instructors recommended which cadets would continue training in single-engine aircraft or begin training in multi-engine planes. The majority of the cadets were sent on to train in multi-engine aircraft. It made sense because bombers, transport, and other twin- and four-engine aircraft required two pilots. Some of the men did not want to fly fighters. They wanted to fly bombers. I wanted to fly a fighter. Those men could have been looking to their post-war future. Civilian airline companies would want pilots with multi-engine experience to fly their passenger planes after the war. Multi-engine experience would also be a factor in hiring a cargo transport pilot. I was recommended for single-engine fighter training.

I was discharged from Walnut Ridge and shipped out to Napier Field, Alabama, for Advanced Training. Napier Field is near Dothan, Alabama, in the southeast corner of the state near the Georgia border.

At Napier Field we learned to use shortwave radio. The cadet was required to master Morse code at 30 words per minute. I also completed instrument tests, and continued to train in the AT-6. It was here that I flew and trained in my first fighter—the P-40N, a single-engine, single-seat, all-metal fighter. The engine produced 1,000 horsepower. It was a quick, nimble fighter that could turn on a dime. The P-40 was flown by the "Flying Tigers," the 1st American Volunteer Group, in China against the Japanese Zero. The plane was also used in North Africa and Europe. I logged a little over 10 hours in the P-40N at Napier Field. It was a fun plane to fly, and I learned to make her dance.

We learned about all of the equipment, including oxygen and safety, and performed routine maintenance on the aircraft. In gunnery ground school we learned about sighting, the harmonics of fixed guns, bombing, and how to clean, disassemble, and reassemble our guns. We learned about communications, tactics, briefing, and critique for flying missions. We also had medical training, and we continued many more hours of physical training (P.T.) and infantry drill.

In January of 1944, I received my wings. Frank, Thelma, Grandma Bailey, and Richie came to the ceremony. I was notified that my parents were at the main gate, and I hopped up and ran to meet them. None of them recognized me as I jogged toward them—no one except Ma, that is.

She told everyone, "That's Billy coming toward us." Frank, Grandma, and Richie disagreed. It had been a while since I had seen them. The Air Corps had grown me up in a hurry. I also weighed 170 pounds and was in the best shape of my life. I kissed Ma and Grandma and hugged my dad and little Richie. It was great to see them. I gave them a tour of the base and we talked about home and my training. I didn't tell them about all of the men who were killed learning to fly. I kept it simple yet interesting for the family.

At that time, there was gas rationing because America needed fuel for the war. Some men from work gave Frank gas coupons so that he could make the trip to see me graduate. We cadets marched in formation and the army band played. The commanding general gave a speech, and we were presented our wings. I was now a second lieutenant—a pilot. I didn't know what or where I'd fly, but I was going to be a fighter pilot...a lifelong dream come true. I was 20 years old.

Cadet Billy D. Kasper with his wings

After graduation, I was given a 10-day leave, so I drove back to Springfield with the family. I went in to National Supply and thanked the men who gave Dad the gas coupons. I drove up to Chicago to see Grandma Kasper and my aunt and uncles. I also stopped by to see my cousin Shirley May and her mother, Alice. Alice was at work and Shirley May, who was nine years old, was alone in her house. She told me that Alice worked a lot of split shifts at the telephone company. "I think she just wants to get away from me," Shirley May said.

"Well, tonight I'm going to take you out to dinner, so get your coat on. It's cold out." I treated her to dinner and we had a real nice time. When I dropped her home after dinner she wanted to cry, but she was a tough little kid. I told her that I would see her when I got home from the war. She gave me a quick hug and then dashed into her house.

I woke up early the next morning and was outside her door when

Shirley May, age 8, in front of Fisk elementary school

Shirley May stepped out on her way to school. "Come on, I'll walk you."

It was bitter cold that day. Shirley May was excited to see me, and bounced up and down and squealed. I walked her to school. She had to stand outside and wait until the school bell rang. The little thing was standing there, shivering. I opened my long winter army coat and she snuggled in with me. Shirley May looked up at me and said, "You're the best, Billy!" The doors opened and the children filed in. We hugged and then Shirley May turned and ran toward the school doors. I rebuttoned my coat and I headed out.

I spent a couple more days at home with the family. The time sure did go by quickly. I liked being home, but I wanted to get back to flying. I wanted to get on with my job. My family drove me to the train station. I had orders to report to Dale Mabry Field in Tallahassee, Florida.

Ma looked me in the eyes, grabbed my cheeks, and said, "I'm not worried about you, Billy. You are gonna come home, and you are going to be fine. I know you can take care of yourself!"

I got a big grin on my face and said, "Hell, Ma, you wouldn't let me play football, but you are okay sending me off to war." I got a big laugh out of that. Ma smiled a sheepish smile and playfully smacked my cheek.

I hugged Frank and Grandma, then Richie. I looked down at Rich and I said, "You know what I'm going to do?"

"What?" Richie asked.

"I am going to name my plane after you."

"Really?"

"You bet. I'll send you a picture."

So, I boarded the train and headed to Dale Mabry Field. I didn't fly in Tallahassee; my job was to wait for orders.

When the orders came, I was to report to a field in Georgia in March to learn to fly the P-39.

"Oh, shit!" I thought. "Of all the fighters, I get the P-39." I did not want to fly that plane. The engine sat behind the pilot and the drive shaft went up between his legs to the propeller. I was always quick to follow orders, but I did not want to fly that damned airplane, so I took my orders in hand and walked up to headquarters. I didn't talk to an officer—this was too important. I went straight to the sergeant's desk. I showed him my orders and asked if he could get them changed so that I could fly a different plane. I didn't push it, I simply made a request. He looked over the orders and said, "I'll see what I can do." I thanked him, turned on my heel, and went back to my room.

Billy D. in Florida during P-51 training

The next day, I had new orders. Report to Bartow Field near Winterhaven and Tampa. I was assigned to learn to fly the P-51. Hot damn!

The P-51 was designed to be an escort fighter. The design of the fighter began around 1939, and the P-51B and C were delivered to England around late 1943. Drop tanks were designed to add vital flying range to fighters. The P-51 equipped with drop tanks and extended range would change the war.

The P-51B and C had a Rolls Royce Merlin V12 engine. The engine developed 1620 horsepower, and had a maximum speed of 439 miles per hour (mph). It would cruise at 325 mph, but in a dive could reach 500 mph. The engine was named after a Merlin, a bird of prey in the falcon family. The P-51 could climb to an altitude of over 41,000 feet, and the range of the plane, with drop tanks, was over 1,000 miles. That range made it capable of flying deep into Germany with the bombers.

The P-51 was 32 feet long and 13.67 feet high, with a wingspan of 37 feet. The plane was armed with four 50-caliber machine guns and carried 1,260 rounds of ammunition. (P-51Ds had six 50-caliber machine guns and carried 1,880 rounds of ammo.) The P-51 could also carry two 500 pound bombs.

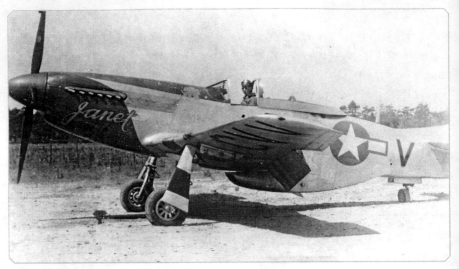

Escort fighter P-51

Much of my training in the P-51 was night flight. I had plenty of opportunities to see what she could do—she was one hell of an aircraft. I was in my element in the P-51. She was like a great lover, powerful and responsive. She was dependable and at the same time, unpredictable.

In World War II, we relied on our vision, and learned to recognize enemy aircraft by sight at long distances. The two fighters that we came up against most often were the Focke-Wulfe FW-190 and the Messerschmidt BF-109. A pilot's life depended on his ability to spot and identify distant aircraft. The pilot who spotted his enemy first could maneuver his plane to gain a tactical advantage.

I flew the P-51A, P-51B, P-51C, and P-51D. I practiced combat formations and target approach. I shot at air and ground targets. Under the threat of court martial, we did not fly in the clouds, because the commanding officer was afraid of air-to-air collisions. I learned the characteristics of the aircraft at different altitudes and how she flew when she had a full load of fuel and was carrying bombs. Fully loaded, the plane weighed 11,000 pounds.

Fighter school taught us to fly like the aerobatic planes at an air show. We learned:

The simple Aileron Roll, where the plane does a full 360-degree revolution on its axis.

The Loop, where you pull back on the stick, invert, then continue back to level flight.

The Break Turn, a hard, flat turn. This is a desperate maneuver used to get out of the way of an attacker's bullets quickly. You start an *Aileron Roll* and follow that with a sharp, backward pull on the stick.

The Immelman Turn, where you make a high-speed pass at a target, then reverses course with a half loop and complete a 180-degree vertical turn.

The Vertical Eight—two consecutive half loops.

The Split S, a half-loop in reverse. You roll the plane inverted, then pull back on the stick—a good attack maneuver when the enemy is at a lower altitude.

The High Yo-Yo, where you pull your fighter into vertical and simultaneously roll the plane and steer it toward the enemy as he tries to escape your initial pass.

There was also the Low Yo-Yo, the Barrel Roll, the Lufberry Circle, Corkscrew, and other various maneuvers. When I was in the cockpit, I was a part of the plane.

One time, while flying at Mabry Field, I came in hot and low over the airfield and rolled to an inverted position. I was so low that I could count the blades of grass. I was pretty damned close to the ground. As I went beyond the field, I followed the contour of the land and my plane dipped out of site. The air officer was so sure I would crash he sent the emergency equipment. Damn, I loved to fly.

When a pilot is that close to the ground, particularly inverted, one little slip and it's all over. Pilots at air shows are not permitted to fly as low as I was; low, level and inverted! I knew what I was doing. When a pilot was flying (on the deck), we said he was cutting the yard or trimming dandelions. If you wanted a plane to gain altitude, you pulled back on the stick or (in bombers) the steering wheel. If the plane was inverted, everything was backwards—you pushed the stick to climb. A pilot could become disoriented and run it in the dirt flying upside down.

While I was in Tallahassee, I met a pretty little blond. Her father owned a restaurant. I would go to town and get myself a room, and on Sunday mornings she would fix me breakfast in her father's restaurant. She was a good kid. One night I was practicing night flying. There were strict rules about flying around populated areas. At a minimum, an altitude of 500 feet would be maintained. That was the rule. There are many hazards at low altitudes in and around cities: buildings, towers, power lines, and more. Knowing where this little blond lived, I decided to say hello. I dove in fast and low, buzzed her house at less than a hundred feet, then headed home in a hurry. I put my fighter down and hurried inside. I grabbed a cup of coffee, opened my log book, and sat down. The officer on duty was yelling, "Who is still out there? I want names! If I catch this smartass who's scaring the population, I'll skin him alive!" I lit a Chesterfield, examined the smoke, and sipped my coffee. That was close. When I saw my girl that weekend, she said that her father had sat straight up in bed. He thought for sure that plane was coming into his bedroom. She said that she knew it was me. When I shipped out, I never wrote that girl. I liked her, but I was going to war and I didn't know if I'd make it back. So, I thought it was better not to write.

Life and Death

Headed to War

While I was in Winterhaven, I met Lester Hovden. Lester and I became quick friends. He played basketball in high school, and was from a small farming community in Ridgeway, Iowa. His family raised milking cows, hogs, and white-faced Herefords. Lester had an older sister and two younger sisters. His father wanted him to take over the family farm, but Les didn't want to be a farmer. He told me that when he worked in the fields, sometimes he would see an airplane fly overhead and he knew he wanted to be a pilot. He wanted to be up there. That was a familiar story for many pilots. I looked out for Les and he looked out for me. Les was a real stand-up guy, a good man. I don't know if I had a better friend during the war.

I made the ocean crossing on a troop transport. It was a Dutch Ship, the New Amsterdam. She was about 700 feet long and had seven or eight deck guns. We crossed the Atlantic without an escort. Officers and enlisted men were separated. We slept in bunks in each quartered area. Having sailing experience, I warned Les not to sleep on the bottom bunk. He asked why. By the end of our first day at sea he found out why and was very happy he listened to me. There were boys hanging over the rail for the whole crossing.

One day, the captain made an announcement. He told us that Allied forces had landed in France—the invasion was on. The mood on the ship was very somber.

The food on ship tasted like shit. We ate the same food as the enlisted men. Close to the end of our passage we (transported officers) found out that the ship's officers were eating pretty damned good. They were living high on the hog. We almost had a mutiny on that ship. A large group of us confronted the captain. We told him that we were officers and we expected the same treatment and food that was due his officers. For the last two days of our nine-day voyage we ate pretty good. He did not want to have a mutiny on his ship.

I landed in Liverpool, England, and was directed to the orientation center. It was here that I learned that the boys who had been flown over got in the D-Day fight. Many of them had already been shot down. I was ready to get into the fight. When you are 20 years old you think that you are invincible. This was what we all had signed up for—we wanted to see some action. There was a large group of new pilots, fighter and bomber pilots, all ready to go to work.

An officer walked into the hall and we snapped to attention. "At ease," he screamed. We sat down at the rectangular tables. The officer paced and told us that we would receive our orders and transportation papers. He gave us a brief overview of the airfields that we would be assigned to, and updated us on the war effort. Then he scanned his audience.

"You are expendable!" he yelled. "Look at the man on your left. Now look at the man on you right." I looked left and then turned to Les. We exchanged smiles. "The men to your left and right will be dead in three months."

I thought, "You son-of-a-bitch!" Unfortunately, I soon learned why he said such a thing. Men were dying by the hundreds.

I was assigned to the 8th Air Force, 67th Fighter Wing, 359th Fighter Group, and 368th Fighter Squadron. The 359th Fighter Group had three squadrons: the 368th, 369th, and 370th. Each squadron had 16 fighters. The 359th Fighter Group's insignia was a unicorn—strength and virtue. The 368th Fighter Squadron's unicorn had a lightning bolt clenched in its mouth.

Each fighter squadron had its own support staff. The fighter squadrons had their own administration, maintenance, ordnance, intelligence, operational support, and flight surgeon. The docs knew the pilots inside out. They had a lot of influence with command. Fighter squadrons were a close-knit group within a close-knit group (the fighter group).

The United States had several numbered Air Forces. The number was associated with the area of the world that an individual Air Force was responsible for:

1st	N.E. U.S.
2nd	N.W. U.S.
3rd	S.E. U.S.
4th	S.W. U.S.
5th	S.W. Pacific
6th	Panama Canal
7th	Central Pacific
8th	England/W. Europe
9th	W. Europe/Mediterranean
10th	China/Burma/India
11th	Alaska
12th	N. Africa/Mediterranean/Europe
13th	W. Pacific
14th	China/Burma/India
15th	Italy/Europe
20th	W. Pacific

From Liverpool, the old coal-fired train took me to Thetford, England. From there, I boarded a truck and headed to East Wretham. The countryside was beautiful, rolling farmlands. Sheep grazed in grassy fields. Les and I and six other men arrived at Wretham Airfield, a grass airfield previously occupied by the Royal Air Force (RAF). I could see trucks and workers gathered at one runway, installing a pierce plank runway. Pierce planking is large rectangular perforated sections of steel. The new runway would give pilots a smoother ride.

Train pulling into Thetford

Wretham was an old English estate. We pulled up to Wretham manor, climbed out of the truck, and my jaw dropped. "WOW! Will you look at that?" The manor was a huge three-story brick and stone building. It had 75 rooms and several fireplaces. This was my new home. The base had hangars and maintenance buildings for aircraft and equipment. There was a briefing hut, a two-story control tower with a fleet of crash and recovery vehicles parked nearby, as well as quarters and a dining hall for the enlisted men. East Wretham was like a village, a small community. It had everything a town of 400 people would need. I told Les that he should be right at home—small town and farm fields.

We were met at Wretham Manor by a captain who informed us that we would be given room assignments and once settled in, we would meet Colonel Tacon, the commander of the 359th Fighter Group.

We entered the manor. Once inside, we were greeted by Flak, a little black mutt. He was the 370th Fighter Squadron's mascot. I was assigned my room, and walked up a grand staircase. The handrail was wide, winding, and made from dark, rich wood. I walked down a carpeted hallway and found my room. I unpacked quickly and had some time, so I toured the manor. It had high ceilings and massive fireplaces surrounded by tiles and wide wood molding. All of the molding in the place was carved, wide, dark wood. The walls were covered with rich wood paneling. There was a large hall for parties and a dining hall for the officers. The place even had its own bar and a Coca-Cola bar. Each squadron had its own lounge and I found the one that be-longed to the 368th pilots.

Wretham Hall

East Wretham only had about a hundred houses. Most of the villag-ers had worked at the manor, which we now occupied. We had bicycles at the base that we could use, and on some of my days off I would go for a ride, weather permitting. I would ride the winding country roads. I enjoyed seeing the houses with thatched roofs and the rolling farm fields. Close by there were 600-year-old ruins to investigate. Or I might ride the six miles to Thetford and have a pint of warm beer before I returned to base.

Some guys at the field were real shutterbugs. I didn't take many pictures. Hell, if I didn't make it home, who was going to describe what or who was in the picture?

I entered the briefing room. Second Lieutenant Hovden was already there. I met a whole slew of other

Tower at Wretham Airfield

second lieutenants, including Barth, Bartlett, Beal, Boyd, Flack, Gordon, and Haas. I grabbed a seat next to Les. Colonel Avelin P. Tacon, Jr. entered the room. We all snapped to attention.

East Entrance to Wretham Airfield

"At ease. Have a seat," Col. Tacon greeted us and welcomed us to the 359th. "I'll get right to it, men. Our primary mission is to provide escort for the heavies. It is our job to protect them from enemy fighters. That means that we will not chase every ME-109 or FW-190 we see. You will maintain escort. You will get between any attacking fighters and the heavies. You will have plenty of opportunities to engage the enemy. If a heavy is damaged, you will stay with that plane until it is safe. The job of an escort is to save lives. I will be watching you, gentlemen. I expect you will do your country proud. You will begin training flights later this week. That is all. Dismissed." Colonel Tacon, or "Hard Tac," as he was called, ran a tight ship. He was a West Point man. We had a job to do, and

Dog and Partridge Pub

he would make sure we followed his rules.

When we were escorting bombers, there might be 300 bombers and 100 to 150 fighters. It would be possible to have 700 fighters escorting more than a thousand bombers.

In 1942, the Allies decided that in order to defeat the Nazis we would have to step up our bombing campaign. We needed to cripple industry and supply lines, and attack all things that supported the enemy's supply lines. The best way to accomplish this, it was decided, was to begin daylight bombing.

B-17 Bomber

In the 1940s, daylight bombing was the most accurate method of attack. The pilots and bombardiers could see their targets. The problem was, the Nazis could see the bombers. Another problem was that at that time, 1942, our fighter escort did not have the range to fly into Germany to protect our bombers.

The most recognized bomber was the B-17, the "Flying Fortress." The plane was manufactured by Boeing, and was so well armed it was called a strategic weapon. It had 13 machine guns that protected the plane from all angles of attack. It was rugged, and could sustain heavy damage and continue to fly. One general said that the plane was so well armed it could defend itself without escort.

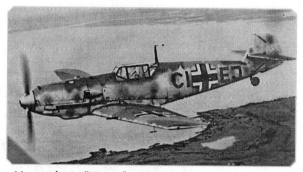

Messerschmitt "Me-109"

However, when the plane was on its bombing run, it had to fly straight and level. The pilot could not take evasive action. This made it a sitting duck for attacking fighters. A B-17 on its bomb run flew slow, straight, and level. Even with its 13 guns, it was a tempting and easy target. The bomber's top speed was 287 mph. Enemy fighters' top speed was between 360 and 400 mph. These small, fast-moving targets were difficult for B-17

65

Focke-Wulf "FW-190"

machine gunners to hit.

The Luftwaffe would wait for our bombers and attack once escort was dropped. On October 14, 1943 during a daylight bombing mission, 60 B-17s were shot down and 138 were damaged. Each B-17 had a crew of 10 men. Many of them did not get out of their ships. It became a priority to press into service a fighter that could protect the bombers to any target deep within Germany and home again. That fighter was the P-51 Mustang. The bomber crews would refer to these fighters as their "Little Friends." Little Friends kept enemy fighters at bay while the Big Friends (Bombers) performed their work.

The B-24, known as "The Liberator," was the most produced aircraft in the Second World War More than half of these aircrafts were manufactured by the Ford Motor Corporation. It could carry a larger bomb load than the

B-24 Liberator

B-17. Fuel tanks throughout the upper fuselage made it a fiery coffin when hit by flak. It was well known for the design of its wings, which were located high on the fuselage. The wing was called the "Davis Wing." Crash landing with this wing design made it much more dangerous than a similar hard landing in a B-17. On land, the high-set wings made the plane act like a person with an inner-ear infection. In a crash landing situation it was almost impossible for the pilot to ease the aircraft to a stop.

The B-24 was a complicated plane to fly, and it took a great amount of skill to do it. B-24 pilots had to work hard to master the aircraft controls. These learned skills paid off in emergency situations. The pilots of B-24s were, at times, able to recover from a spin—almost unheard of from such a large aircraft. B-17s did not recover from a spin.

Seventy Missions

July, 1944

July 4, 1944, I was back up in the air in a P-51B. I only flew for one training hour. For the next few days we practiced. We practiced escort procedures and landings. We learned how to form up in columns, the 359th way, preparing to fly out in formation. We practiced dive bombing. We practiced strafing: come in low and fast. We made one pass on a train if it had steam up. If it didn't, we made a pass, then circled and went at it again if he had steam up. The idea was that you wanted the boiler on the train to be at full pressure. When the boiler was up and you hit it with your .50s, it would explode like fireworks on the fourth of July.

When we were at work (on a mission), each fighter squadron had its own call sign. The 368th was Jigger, the 369th was Tinplate, and the 370th was Red Cross. I flew in the 368th, so I might be Blue Jigger. The colors represented the flight (four aircraft) within the squadron. I won't use the call signs when I tell you about a mission since they were really just important to us, the pilots.

Strafing tactics would be used on any ground targets and, of course, on enemy airfields. The Army Air Corps developed strafing tactics in the spring of 1944. The Nazi fighters had been reluctant to come up and take us on. They were saving themselves for our bombers, so Major General William

Kepner decided we should take the fight to them. If they wouldn't come up, we would hit them while they were parked on their airfields. The general recruited volunteers to learn, practice, and eventually teach strafing to all fighter groups. The group would become known as "Bill's Buzz Boys." Four men from the 359th Fighter Group volunteered. They were Lieutenants John Oliphant, Robert Thacker, and Clifford Carter, and Captain Charles Ettlesen, a West Point man who was selected as flight leader of the volunteer group. During this training, Carter was killed by flak.

Ettlesen was shot down during a mission in May 1944. He was able to bail out of his aircraft, and the rumor was that he evaded capture and was working with the French Resistance. In June, Oliphant was shot down, and was also said to be working with the French Resistance. Oliphant's mother, however, received a KIA notice, because those who witnessed the crash were sure he was dead. Later, it was confirmed that he was, indeed, alive. Thacker eventually completed his tour of duty and was shipped home.

In the month of June I had my crew chief assigned to me—Staff Sergeant Charles Doersom. A man can be the best pilot in the outfit, but if he doesn't have a top-notch crew chief, then he'll just end up dead. Chuck was a top-of-the-line mechanic and engine man. I liked talking engines with him. He grew up in Gettysburg, Pennsylvania. His father owned an airport in Gettysburg, so Chuck grew up around planes. He repaired and rebuilt airplane engines even as a young teenager. He also knew his way around a sewing machine. In the 1930s, many planes were constructed of wood with fabric stretched over the wooden frame. When the fabric tore, it had to be sewn, so Chuck learned to sew. He took pride in his work. Chuck could fly, but he preferred to keep his feet on the ground. A plane in his charge was in good hands. I was very fortunate. All I had to do was fly the thing. No worries.

We continued to use the Link Trainer as part of our training. Operators could easily observe our actions in the trainer. They could spot potential problems with the pilot and take any required action

Combat was a fight or a struggle...a purposeful, violent struggle. The purpose was to dominate the opposition. Kill or be killed. If a man remembered his training and listened to that little voice in his head, he might live to go home and see his family. While you were doing your job, you didn't think about dying. You were focused on the mission at hand. A person who thought about dying would probably get himself killed. Fear could paralyze a man. Someone put it this way, "You have to fly as if you are already dead." He meant that if you had already reached your destination, then you wouldn't worry about the journey.

Don't get me wrong—everyone got scared...a little water down the leg. What counted was what you did when you got scared. You could use the fear and fight for your life, or let the fear overcome you and...die. When you are driving your car and some idiot swerves into your lane, do you throw your hands up and scream or do you take evasive action and try to save yourself? When I was a kid, Frank would always say, "Be ready to act if someone runs a stop or something. Think ahead and plan. Anticipate."

That's how I flew. I surveyed my surroundings and asked myself, 'How can I gain an advantage over enemy aircraft? Are there clouds I could duck into?' It was necessary for me to keep my eyes open, so I wouldn't get bounced and give an enemy fighter an advantage. Getting bounced is when a pilot is surprised by the enemy from above or behind. A pilot applied his knowledge, training, and experience to a situation. A split-second decision could mean the difference between life and death. We weren't playing paddy cake up there. Sometimes I had to anticipate where I could put the plane down if it was hit or if I encountered mechanical problems.

On July 16, my name was up for the next day's mission. I slept pretty good that night. I was ready to go do the job that I had trained so much for. I don't know if I was nervous, but I was ready.

July 17, 1944, was my first mission...a nighttime mission. We were to provide escort for bombers. The mission took us to Montdidier near Paris, France. Forty-nine Mustangs took off and seven aborted—machines break. On this mission, no planes were lost and no enemy aircraft were encountered.

The toughest thing about a night mission was the wait. It was like going on your first date. You woke up early in the morning, got dressed, ate... and then what? Take-off wasn't until after 6:30 pm, or 1830. It was July, so we had sunlight until 9:00 or 9:30 pm. We rendezvoused with the bombers at 8:10, or 2010. The mission was under M.E.W. Control, which meant that ground radar stations directed the bombers and fighters to the target.

The sun was setting on our return flight. We were flying directly into the orange, blue-gray sunset. As night closed in, the exhaust from our fighters was quite a sight. Balls of fire caused by the controlled explosions in the engines' combustion chambers lit up the sky around the nose of the aircraft. I was flying behind several other P-51s. From where I sat, it looked like flashing torches streaking through the night sky. We touched down at 11:30 pm. It would be a short night for me; I had to get up at 5:30 am for my second mission. After we landed, we headed to debriefing, where I told what I saw, what I did, and things I remembered about the mission.

Doc Dunnebier

Next, it was time to talk to the doc. The 368th's flight surgeon was Doc Dunnebier. He would check our heart, blood pressure, and ask questions to determine our mental well-being. My pulse was 65 beats per minute. My blood pressure was 108 over 60. My head was still square on my shoulders. After my check-up, the doc pulled out a bottle of whiskey and poured out a nice tall shot for me, and told me to go ahead and have a drink. I studied the glass and asked him what that was for? Doc said that it was to calm my nerves. I told him that I thought my nerves were already pretty calm.

He picked up the glass and carefully poured the whiskey back in to the bottle. "You don't have to drink it, Lieutenant. Is it for religious reasons that you don't want it?"

I laughed and said, "Oh, hell no, sir. It's just that my nerves feel pretty good. I don't think I need to be calmed down. Can I save up those shots until I have enough for a bottle?"

Doc Dunnebier paused and thought for a second. He looked at me over his glasses. Thinking out loud he said, "Hmm, no one ever asked me

B-17 Bomber with P-51 escort

that before." He removed his glasses, stared at the ceiling, and rubbed his eyes as he thought. "I don't see why not. Okay, both of us will keep track and when you have saved up enough, I'll give you a bottle."

After the other pilots got word of what I was doing, they started saving their shots. Almost everyone in the 368th was saving up for a bottle. We were going to have quite a little party after everyone saved up for their bottle.

I woke up at 5:30 the morning of June 18, 1944. I looked out the window—overcast. I always liked to shower and shave in the evening. That way, all I had to do in the morning was jump into my clothes and run a comb through my hair. Next, I'd head out for breakfast and my first cup of coffee. I'd sit with Les and some of the other men in the 368th. After I ate, it was time for a Chesterfield and another cup of coffee. Then, it was time to head for the trucks—well, after a pit stop, that is. I still had time for another smoke before the trucks left for the briefing room. While standing there, I would talk to the fellas about the weather, where we might go, and small talk. Our talk and our laughs would rise to a nervous pitch. Some guys would say, "I'm gonna get one today" or "Bring 'em on"...things like that. I would feel the nerves. Everyone was nervous. We never talked about it, but you could tell. Some guys got real quiet. I think we all went to the bathroom with greater frequency.

Before you knew it, it was time to roll. We climbed into the trucks, and it was off to the briefing room. Everyone took a seat and "Stormy," our weatherman, kicked off the briefing. "Today, gentlemen, it is going to be 10/10 (cloudy and overcast) all the way in and all the way out." I could hear some guys moan. I just never really reacted to weather. Like every-

Men praying outside before a mission

one else, I liked clear skies and good visibility, but the weather is what it is...I couldn't wave a wand and change it. Besides, sometimes you could encounter more turbulence on a clear day. So, okay, 10/10. I was ready for that. Now, what about the map? The map laid out our route to the target, rendezvous with the bombers, and the route home. We were headed to Herde, Denmark, which had synthetic oil plants and storage facilities. Flak was anticipated in and out. We were escorting B-17s, and I was assigned to fly close support. Colonel Tacon was leading this mission, so everyone would be on their best behavior. The colonel expected tight formations. Our columns looked as straight as soldiers in formation. We were to get into formation quickly after take-off, hit our marks, be on time, and stay with the bombers until released.

The briefing ended. I knew my job, where I was going, and who I was following. We crowded outside for the chaplain's prayer. Why did we pray outside? It wasn't always that way. The prayers used to be in the briefing room. One day, a chaplain said some prayers there and told the pilots to be ready to "Meet Your Maker." It was his "you are going to die today" prayer, and the pilots—every single one of them—refused to fly. When the commanding general found out about this, he hit the ceiling. He called Colonel Tacon and raised hell...one of those conversations where you hold the phone away from your ear. After the general stopped yelling and demanding that heads roll, Col. Tacon said his piece. He pointed out that the chaplain was in the briefing room, where everything said is fact as is known regarding the mission. The chaplain told the men they would die if they went up that day. He was transferred back to the States, and from then on, prayers were held outside.

This chaplain asked for God's protection in this dangerous struggle that we were about to enter into. The seriousness of our business was clear to us all. "Amen," the chaplain finished, and "Amen" was what we replied. Let's go to work.

Next, we headed to the pilot's shack, where our equipment was waiting for us: flying suit, helmet, Mae West life jacket, and parachute. The Mae West was our inflatable personal flotation device. It got its name because when a pilot wears it, he looks as well-endowed as the actress.

After that, it was time for S-2 (intelligence). Here, I checked my pockets and handed over my wallet. Nothing with personal writing could go in the plane. I showed my dog tags, because no one flies without dog tags. We didn't want the Gestapo to execute us as a spy. Dog tags identified us as a combatant. If captured, we should be treated according to the rules set forth in the Geneva Convention. *Should be.* I took my escape kit and put it, the course card, and the map in my pocket.

Next stop: my plane. I imagine it would be embarrassing for the pilot who didn't check to see where his plane was parked. We didn't put little flags on the antennas. Can you picture a pilot running around asking, "Have you seen my plane?" On this particular day I was flying a "B" model. We had "Bs," "Cs" and "Ds." The "B" and "C" had canopies like a P-47. The canopy followed the line of the aircraft and had steel ribs. It carried four .50-caliber machine guns. The "D" had a bubble canopy, designed to give the pilot a clear 360-degree view. There were no canopy supports to obstruct the pilot's view. It also had six .50-caliber machine guns. It never really mattered to me which P-51 I was flying. I was flying, and that's what mattered to me.

Some of the men put cotton in their ears because of the cockpit noise in the aircraft. It can be pretty noisy in a P-51. I never put cotton in my ears, unless I had an earache. I wanted to tune my ears into the mechanical workings of the engine. When I drove a car, I left the radio off for the same reason.

When we left S-2 for our planes, no one said good-bye or shook hands. We just checked our watches and walked toward our planes.

Billy D. and Sergeant Doerson, chief mechanic

I walked to my plane the same way I would walk through the gate at National Supply. Just another work day. Sergeant Doerson was waiting at the plane for me and smiled as I approached. He was a good man. I was glad he was my chief.

"I hope that smile means you had a good night." Ground crews worked all night on the aircraft and worried all day while we are gone.

"I did have a good night," he replied as I handed him my helmet.

"How is she running?"

"Purring like a kitten, sir."

As we talked, I walked around the plane, looking her over and giving her a visual inspection. I climbed on the wing, Doerson behind me, and slithered into the cockpit. It was real cozy in the cockpit. It's a damned good thing I weighed 175 pounds. Ten more pounds and I would have needed a can of grease and a shoe horn to get me in...then it would take a crane to hoist me back out. Once I was in the cockpit, I squirmed and wriggled around until I was comfortable. Then, I fastened the dinghy to the chute (the dinghy always stayed in the aircraft). Next, I fastened my crash straps.

I had better be comfortable at this point, because when the straps were tightened, I was stuck. I would be in that position the entire mission. Once strapped in, I put on my helmet, clamped my oxygen hose to the straps, tested the oxygen, plugged in and turned on the radio, set the trim for take-off, set the gyro compass, set the altimeter, gun heat and pitot heat on (pitot is the instruments' heat), and set the plane's clock to my watch.

I checked the brakes and set the flap handle in the "up" position. By setting the flap handle, the flaps would automatically come to the up position when the engine fires. Flaps were up for take-off. Doerson closed my canopy and I locked it. One more check of the instruments and I shouted, "Chocks out." I paused as I looked side to side and yelled, "Clear!"

I reached down and turned on the battery, ignition switch, fuel pump, and gas line. I primed the engine and hit the starter button. It was a warm day. She spit and sputtered and came to life on the first try. The whole aircraft shook as she woke up, then the RPMs settled and she purred like a kitten—a really big kitten. Yes, it was loud when the P-51's Merlin came to life. Exhaust fumes filled the air and crept into the cockpit through my side sliding window. I loved that smell. I switched off the starter and set the fuel mixture.

It was my turn to taxi. I checked the engine instruments, flaps, and brakes, then rolled her out of the parking space and into line. While I waited, I did my final engine checks. I ran up the RPMs and then idled her. She sounded great. I rolled to take-off position and closed the sliding window on the canopy. I was in my office and ready to get down to work. The nerves were long gone. I don't know when the nerves left me.

I turned up the fuel boost and put the throttle to the wall. She rolled down the runway, picking up speed in a hurry. I bounced up and down on the grass runway. Thousands of take-offs in all kinds of weather had taken their toll on the grass runway. Installation of the pierce plank runway when completed would eventually smooth out the ride, but at the moment, I was bouncing along. I reached take-off speed and pulled back on the stick. The Earth released her grip on the plane and we were up. I liked that feeling in my stomach when I lifted off. Free of Earth, I rapidly climbed and got into formation. My flight was in the middle of the formation—four planes to a flight.

We headed outbound in formation. I heard an abort called from one of the pilots, then another. Just two aborts. Flights changed as aircraft moved up to fill the two open positions. The forward most flights were kept full—four planes. This meant that a flight at the back of the pack could end up with just one plane. Our strength was now 40 P-51s. Colonel Tacon called, "Tighten it up! Tighten it up!"

The mission was scheduled to last four hours. Four or five hours was a long time to sit in a P-51 cockpit. I couldn't just get out and stretch my legs. Some pilots, sitting alone in their cockpits, talked to themselves. They yelled, screamed and pumped their fists, sang, growled, or hummed. It could be pretty entertaining to watch a pilot throwing a fit or singing in their cockpit. I didn't do too much of that. I just tried to stay on my toes, eyes scanning the sky. I listened to the engine and watched the instruments. I sometimes would talk to the aircraft. I might tell my plane how good she sounded and how pretty she looked. I never talked to her in a mean voice. Sometimes, I would talk to her in my John Wayne voice, "Well, you sure sound good, little Missy." Usually, though, I just observed my surroundings.

We cleared the coast and moved out over the water, keeping up our speed. There was the enemy coast. We spread out into battle formation. We were few in numbers, protecting the Big Friends. We rendezvoused with the heavies. I moved around in the bomber's contrail, all the time listening for calls over the radio that alerted us to enemy fighters and mission updates. The weather was crappy. We encountered flak, but it was not accurate. The B-17s dropped their bombs. Results couldn't be observed because of the cloud cover. I hoped the bombers were a lot more accurate than the German flak. No enemy fighters were encountered...I guess the weather was too crappy for them. Everyone returned to base safely. Two missions under my belt. My bottom sure was sore when I climbed out of the cockpit.

Billy D. taken on July 19, 1944 just after flying a mission to Munich, Germany—tired young man

The next day, July 18, 1944, I was up again. Things heated up a little more on this mission. The target was Munich, Germany. Fifty-two of us took-off and 15 aborted. Flak was heavy, and we lost 11 B-17s. I saw one bomber get hit by flak and it immediately spun toward Earth. I didn't see any chutes.

A couple ME-109s dove through our formation. They did not fire a shot. They just dove through us and headed for the deck. The flight leader radioed, "Hold your position, everyone. They are trying to lure us away so their friends can bounce the heavies." We maintained escort. We wouldn't want to get drawn away and have a larger force attack the B-17s.

We returned to base after another long mission. Les walked over to me and said, "Farming might not be so bad after all." We had a good laugh over that one.

On July 20, 1944, we escorted B-17s to Leipzig, Germany. The target was the oil industry. Fifty-four of us took off; 17 aborted. The 368th was flying close support and the 370th was flying top support. Top support flew high above everyone else. The planes flying top support protected the bombers from getting jumped (from above). It was quite a sight when you flew top cover. You looked down on hundreds of bombers and fighters flying in formation, bomber streams trailing the parade and the Earth far below. The formation was spread out over miles of sky.

Two B-17s were damaged by flak. The bombers turned to limp for home. Two P-51s from the 368th Fighter Squadron stayed with them until they were clear of any danger from enemy fighters. Meanwhile, ME-109s attacked some heavies from the rear. Five bombers quickly went down... only one chute was observed, even though the B-17 had a crew of 10. The 370th dove after the enemy aircraft and scored one kill and one probable. The 370th, however, lost one pilot.

July 23, 1944, we escorted B-24s to Juvincourt, France. No bombers or fighters were lost. The cloud cover was thick. Bombing results could not be observed. Enemy fighters usually wouldn't come up when the cloud cover was as thick as it was that day.

A weather front came in and stalled, making the weather too bad for flying. With the time off, we spent some time on indoor activities. We played ping pong and cards, drank at the bar, read, or listened to the radio. We got restless staying inside. Les, Bartlett, Wiley,

Messerschmitt Me163A Rocket Interceptor

and I, along with a few other guys, rode bicycles to Thetford. We walked around the village and found a pub, where we drank some warm beer and had a few laughs.

July 28, 1944, we escorted B-17s to Merseburg, Germany. About the time I was stepping outside to head to breakfast, bombers flew overhead on their way to Germany. Colonel Tacon led this flight. The target at Merseburg was the oil industry. Merseburg had a vast oil complex, which was a high-priority target. We were an hour away from the target when two B-17s got too close. They just drifted right into each other, and one of them exploded. The explosion was thunderous—the sky shook. A huge fireball flashed out of billowing black smoke. Pieces of the plane flew out of the giant fire ball. The other bomber went down in a spin. Only three chutes were seen. South of Merseburg, Col. Tacon called "Bandits" at 6 o'clock high. What he saw were German jet fighters, the ME-163. His was the first sighting of a Nazi jet aircraft. The jets made a run at the B-17s. We put the throttle to the wall and positioned ourselves between them and the bombers. The jets aborted their attack and streaked off out of sight.

On July 29, 1944, we flew escort to Bremen, Germany. The cloud cover was 10/10. Flak was heavy but inaccurate because of the overcast skies. Fifty-three P-51s took off; 16 aborted. On our return flight we were informed that weather conditions had deteriorated, visibility was poor. Twenty-seven pilots landed at other bases on the continent. Ten of us landed at East Wretham. We were flying on instruments. I started my final approach. The airport landing beacon was on. The runway lined up, but I couldn't see a thing. I approached the runway...altitude 500 feet, 400 feet, 300 feet, 200 hundred feet. I gave it full throttle, pulled back on the stick, and swung around for another approach. I don't know why I did it. That little voice in my head told me to go around again, and I always listened to that little voice. I lined up the runway a second time...altitude 500 feet, 400 feet, 300 feet, 200 feet, 100 feet, 50 feet. I pulled back on the stick and feathered the landing.

After debriefing, I sat down in the hall with a cup of coffee and a smoke. I was sipping my coffee and talking to some of the fellas when a lieutenant stepped in and in a loud voice said, "Who was flying cv-v106949?"

I hollered back to him, "That would be me."

He walked over, smiled, slapped me on the back, and sat down. He looked at me, then the others at the table and said, "I was making my final approach, trying to find the runway through the shit. Then, out of nowhere, another P-51 was right on top of me. I could have reached up and polished his wheels. I thought I was dead for sure. Then the engine roared and the plane pulled up and banked left and it disappeared. The plane was so close I read cv-v106949. Kasper, that was close. I don't know why you pulled up when you did, but you saved both our lives. Why did you pull up?"

I took a drag on my Chesterfield, looked him in the eye, and said, "A voice in my head said, 'Pull up now!' I never saw your plane. Call it what you want—a feeling, a little voice, whatever. I always listen to that inner voice."

"Keep listening, brother—keep listening," he said.

Later that day, we got the word that Flight Officer Wiley's plane went down. He was taken prisoner. He would spend the rest of the war in a stalag.

Every month we had a general briefing. Reports were made about anything that impacted the fighter group—maintenance issues, supplies and inventory levels, man hours spent on repairs, and so on. We discussed the group's strength, the number of planes available. The flight surgeon gave his report on the health of the group, which he reported as excellent. No new cases of venereal disease. Citations were handed out. New arrivals were introduced and goodbyes were said to those who had completed their tours.

AUGUST, 1944

August 1, 1944, the 359th flew escort for B-17s. They dropped supplies to the free French in southern France. The mission was uneventful, except Lieutenant Beal was forced to land in Normandy. His plane developed engine trouble, and he spent the night in a foxhole while the Germans bombed the airfield. The next day, the ground crew changed out the engine in his P-51 and he flew back to East Wretham.

On August 2, 1944, we escorted B-17s. The target was fuel dumps near Paris. Fifty-five P-51s took off; 18 aborted. The mechanics at the base complained about the aborts. After testing the aborted aircraft, they found that only ten percent of them had a mechanical problem. The mechanics were frustrated that checking for problems in these aircraft took them away from other duties. In July and August the mechanics were testing and prepping the new P-51Ds for action. Troubleshooting the aborted aircraft cost them several man hours that could have been spent on the new aircraft.

Flying a fighter was dangerous business. A pilot had to have confidence that his aircraft would carry him to and from the battle without mechanical problems. I suppose a fella could start hearing a lot of things when he was headed into battle.

After escort was dropped, we went strafing. Captain Hawkinson of the 368th led white flight after some trucks. Strafing was the most dangerous action a fighter could take. Hawkinson went in low and fast. When a plane was strafing, it was vulnerable to small arms fire (rifles, machine guns, and pistols), as well as anti-aircraft and armored vehicle fire. One bullet in the coolant line could bring a P-51 down. A strafing pilot also had to watch out for power lines and poles. Pieces of metal from exploding trains and trucks also brought down fighters. When we came in low and fast, we hoped we could get past the target before the enemy could get a bead on us.

Cpt. Hawkinson fired on the trucks when he was 400 yards out. The Nazis' anti-aircraft scored hits on his P-51. He was able to get enough altitude to bail out. When he landed, he broke his ankle and crawled to a hedgerow for cover. A German patrol was sent out to search for him, and came within four feet of his hiding place. He stayed in the hedgerow until the Germans left the area. When he was sure no enemy troops were in the vicinity, he crawled out of his hiding place. Eventually, he found a friendly Frenchman who hid him in a barn. He stayed there until the Allies pushed the Germans out of the area.

Captain Hawkinson was our only casualty. We returned to Wretham and took our turns landing. Second Lieutenant Holloman made his approach. The tower saw that his right-side landing gear did not lower, so they waived him off. He circled the field to burn off fuel and made several attempts to lower the landing gear. All other fighters landed, then the crash trucks drove into position. It was Holloman's turn. We all stood and watched as he made his approach. Gently, he set the left wheel down. He kept the plane up on that wheel and, slowly, the right side of the aircraft lowered until it rubbed the ground. He slid in with minimal damage to the aircraft. It was a textbook landing. We broke out into applause, hoots, and hollers. Good job, Holloman.

On August 3, 1944, we escorted B-24 bombers to Paris. Cloud cover was heavy, so the bombers went after alternative targets. The escort was routine; no bombers were lost. We returned to base. A P-51 crashed on landing and the pilot scrambled to safety. Next, Lieutenant Colonel Murphy made his approach. He touched down and as he rolled down the runway, he applied his brakes. The brakes locked up and the plane nosed over and ended upside-down. Murphy was unhurt and his aircraft was repaired. Never a dull moment.

August 8, 1944, we escorted bombers to Caen, France. The target that day was marshalling yards, locations where railroad tracks came together from different directions to form a rail yard. The rail yard had side tracks where empty and loaded cars waited to hitch a ride with a locomotive. At a marshalling yard there were warehouses and loading docks filled with supplies for the enemy. There was also a high concentration of troops heading to and from the battle front. If we could destroy or cause severe damage to a marshalling yard, the enemy would be without supplies needed to wage war. We could also cause a high number of casualties. A successful attack could make it difficult for the enemy to bring up reinforcements from the rear. Fewer enemy troops trying to kill our boys. A hungry, ill-equipped army was much more vulnerable than a well-equipped, reinforced fighting unit.

The bombers hit their targets that day and inflicted a great deal of damage on the Nazis. The 368th dropped escort. We went hunting. Lieutenant Keesey was leading my flight; I flew his wing. We spotted 25 FW-190s below us at 3,000 feet. The four of us peeled off and dove down after them. They quickly shot up to 15,000 feet. The chase was on. We followed them through the clouds. I squeezed a couple rounds off as we closed in on them. Then, from above and behind, we were bounced by 30 FW-190s.

Lieutenant John Allen was hit immediately and went down with his plane. I did an aileron roll and quickly pulled back on the stick. Tracers were above and below me. We were in a fight, now! The maneuver I used is one that is only used when you are surprised from the rear. One drawback to the move is you lose a lot of speed. I rolled right into a cloud. I got my speed up and came out of the clouds firing. I got hits on one enemy aircraft (e/a) and turned on another that was diving after a P-51. I gave him a squirt and he changed course. I tagged another that I was sure was a kill.

Two FW-190s got on my tail. Tracers shot over my cockpit. I pushed the nose down and entered a steep dive. They followed. I pulled out of the dive. They were still on my tail. Another FW-190 was headed toward me from 9:00 high. I ducked into the clouds. I flew in and out of the clouds, changing course several times. I popped out of the clouds and scanned the sky. No enemy aircraft. I headed for home, but stayed on my toes. No enemy aircraft.

I eventually rejoined Lt. Keesey. He downed one of the FW-190s. I was not credited with a kill, or a probable. That's okay. I was still in one piece. It was one hell of a fight. Welcome to France, Bill. Lieutenant Cherry of the 368th was also shot down. He survived with severe burns, but was taken prisoner.

August 10, 1944, we headed to Strasbourg, France, to do a little strafing and dive bombing. We were very excited to be able to cut loose and raise some hell. Forty-nine Mustangs took off and only two aborted. Each plane carried two 500-pound bombs. Our target was the marshalling yards at Bishwiller. Flight by flight, we dove in, scoring hits on buildings, locomotives, tracks, railroad cars, and trucks. Lester Hovden's flight made the run, and I was in the flight right behind him. Les dove to 8,000 feet and made a quick 45-degree turn to line up the target. The nose of his P-51 rose slightly and then his wings folded up and came off. Gasoline sprayed the plane, but it did not catch fire. The Mustang disintegrated as it sped toward the ground. I couldn't believe the sight before my eyes. My flight altered its course. We didn't want to take the chance of dropping bombs on Les—he might have survived. It appeared he was able to get the nose up, so he didn't nose in. There was no explosion. Maybe he survived the impact. I would not report him killed in action. I knew, though, that he was dead. His wings fell off! There was a lot of screaming and swearing over the radio. The 368th rolled up to cover the other squadrons while the 369th pressed the attack. Lieutenant McCluskey was shot down and killed while strafing. We caused a lot of damage that day, but we lost two men. No one in our squadron made any claims. I think everyone was shook up. Everyone had lost friends, but not that way. Wings don't just fall off.

Back when we had first arrived and that S.O.B. had us look to the right and to the left, I never thought that Les would be one of those who would be dead within a month. I now fully understood what he meant that day. War is a deadly business.

Just the night before the mission, Les and I had been looking over the planes. Neither one of us had an aircraft that was our own yet. I was assigned a "C" and Les was assigned a "B." Les said that he would like to fly the newer "C." I told him to take it, I didn't care. He said, "No, it's yours."

We went back and forth and finally I said, "Okay, I'll flip you for it." He agreed and I pulled out a coin, "Call it."

He called "Heads" as I flipped the coin. It fell to the ground. Tails faced up. I won the toss.

I said, "Go ahead and take it anyway, Les."

He refused. "You won fair and square. It's all yours."

So, Les flew the P-51B August 10, 1944. The investigation into his crash concluded that Lt. Hovden put too much strain on the airframe when he made the quick 45-degree turn. The aircraft could not take the quick turn while carrying the bombs. That was that, and they closed the books on the incident. No one in the fighter group had ever seen wings come off like that, but I let it go. I did not protest. I had to keep my head on straight—I had missions to fly. I would never forget Les. He was a good man, and I was proud to have known him.

Lester W. Hovden

After that, everyone demanded that the wings on the planes be checked. As you can imagine, there was quite an uproar. So, the wings were checked for proper mounting, possible stress fractures, and metal fatigue.

The 359th stood down August 11, 1944.

On August 12, 1944, we flew escort to Metz, France. Bombing results were good. Lieutenant Gordon from the 368th had to make an emergency landing in Normandy, but his engine was quickly repaired and he made it back home before nightfall.

Meanwhile, the runway overhaul at East Wretham continued. Workers were laying down the steel pierce plank runway. To install the pierce plank, the workers had to fill ruts and holes. The fill was packed tight, and the ground was leveled. After that was done, the steel was laid down and the individual planks were secured and bolted together. Work on the runways proceeded at a slow pace. It seemed to us, the pilots, that there was a lot more talking and smoking cigarettes than work.

August 13, 1944, we were going strafing. In the briefing, we were given the latest intelligence. We examined photos, maps, and contour lines, and discussed known anti-aircraft emplacements. Each flight was given an axis of attack. The attack had to be coordinated so we could inflict maximum damage. We used an epidiascope (optical projector) to diagram and organize the attack, which would be carried out in layers. The attacking fighter squadron would fly at 4,000 feet. When the target was in sight, the attacking aircraft would dive, reaching speeds of 450 to 500 miles per hour. The attacking squadron would open fire at 300 to 400 yards distance from the target. If the target was a train or truck, we would open up at 1,000 yards since those could be carrying ammunition. We didn't want the explosion to knock us down. Fighters had been downed by exploding trucks and trains. We would come in low (treetop or lower). Speed and following the contour of the Earth were our allies. We would hit the target and continue terrain following until out of range of the defenders. Then, we would regain altitude and swing around for another pass.

Another fighter squadron would fly at 5,000 feet and the third squadron at 8,000 feet. The top cover groups would protect the attacking squadron, so they didn't get bounced by enemy aircraft. The attacking squadron's focus would be down, aiming for the ground targets, while the top scanned the sky for enemy aircraft. The attacking squadron would make a couple passes. The group would then swing up and assume the top cover position. The top cover group would drop to 5,000 feet, and the group that had previously been at 5,000 feet would become the attacking squadron. It was like an aerial ballet. We had never been bounced using this technique.

Colonel Tacon was very straightforward. He didn't candy-coat things. He would tell anyone, "If you do it (strafe) enough, you are bound to get it in the end." If you go to the well so many times you are bound to get wet. Armed with that knowledge, we still got excited when we had the opportunity to strafe.

Our target that day was the rail system in Paris. We also carried bombs. The 368th went in first. We hit tracks, locomotives, storage units, trucks, railroad cars, and we put a big closed sign on a railroad tunnel. We all went to the well that day and no one got wet.

August 14, 1944, our target was Stuttgart, Germany. We escorted B-17s. Their target was airfields. Bombing results were good. We were in France on our return trip when we broke escort. We were hunting targets of opportunity.

We strafed trains, trucks, and boxcars. I got a staff car—I hope a Nazi general was in that car. We were near Commerce, France. We made a pass at some railway targets. Out of the corner of my eye I spotted a staff car in the middle of a little French town. I swung around and

Installing a steel plank runway

got him in my sights. I was heading downtown and trimming dandelions. He saw me and was speeding in the opposite direction.

The Air Corps didn't encourage pilots to fly downtown and window shop. Many things could go wrong. The obvious concern was hitting a building. If someone had opened a door or window, my wing would have ripped their arm off. I had little room for error. In town there were power lines and poles—at 450 mph, a wire could jump out at you. Downtown you were also likely to encounter small-arms fire. I was moving so fast, though, that I wasn't worried about a soldier getting a bead on me.

Three-hundred yards from the staff car, I gave him a squirt. My .50-caliber machine guns literally cut that staff car in half. The car exploded. No survivors in that pile of junk. If there was a general in the car, I hoped he was a close friend of Hitler's.

When I returned from the mission I saw what was left of a B-24 (Liberator) in a field about 200 yards from the base. It didn't look good for anyone who was in it. As it turned out, there were no casualties.

On August 16, 1944, we escorted B-17s to Böhlen, Germany. The targets were oil industry, an airfield, and aircraft industry. The 370th flew top cover. Lieutenant Colonel Murphy spotted contrails heading toward a struggling B-17. It was a ME-163 jet, a Komet. Murphy attacked and hit it. The top of the fuselage blew off from the .50-caliber strikes. Murphy had just scored

P-51's providing escort

the first shoot-down of a 163 Komet. His wingman, Lieutenant Jones, went after a second Komet. Shortly after Murphy scored his kill, Jones scored the second kill of a Komet. A great day for the 359th.

August 18, 1944, we were escorting B-17s to St. Dizier, France. Fifty of use took off and there were no aborts. After we dropped escort, we did some strafing. The 369th found an airfield and strafed it. They destroyed five planes on the ground and damaged a few more. Lieutenant Melrose was hit by flak and listed MIA. Lieutenant Burtner was also hit by flak. He bailed out. We got word that Patton's boys picked him up.

Strafing after we dropped escort was different than a "strafing mission." We had strafing maps that identified possible targets of opportunity, but the flight leaders were in charge of their individual flight's actions. The attack was not as organized and there was no top cover. Lieutenant Williams was killed August 17th while strafing trucks. He was bounced by four FW-190s. No top cover.

I woke up August 19th and looked out the window. I couldn't see a hundred feet. "Stormy" said that we would be socked in for at least three days. The 368th decided that this was a great opportunity for a party. We found Doc and collected our whiskey bottles. We had quite a party. We even had a band. One fella did a comedy bit and really had us howling. I liked a good laugh. I thought it was good to let your hair down sometimes. I toasted the "happy life."

Later that evening, after a lot of whiskey, I decided that I needed to get some air—you know, to sober up a little. I needed to walk it off. I went outside to get some fresh air. I was on my second lap around the manor house when I ran into Colonel Tacon. "Oh, shit," I thought. I snapped to attention and saluted. I am sure I was swaying as I stood there.

The colonel returned my salute. "At ease, Kasper," he said. "What are you doing out here this time of night?"

"Well, sir," I began, "I had a little too much to drink tonight and I thought I would come out here and get some fresh air. You know, sober up.

"Is it working?"

"I think I am sobering up pretty fast right now, sir."

"Can you tell me one thing, Kasper?"

"Yes, sir?" I replied, thinking, "Where the hell is this going?"

"Where are your pants, Kasper?"

"Shit!" I looked down. I was standing there in my boxers. I said the only thing I could say, "They are in my room, sir."

Colonel Tacon stood there a minute, processing the scene. Then, he raised his eyebrow and said, "Carry on." We saluted and he walked off into the night. I made my way back to my room. I missed breakfast. I think a lot of men missed breakfast.

The weather cleared and August 24, 1944, we were back to work. We escorted B-17s to Weimar, Germany. On our way back home, Lieutenants Barth and Britton (368th) strafed a locomotive and an armed trawler.

P-51s were able to escort bombers to Germany and back because of the invention of drop tanks, very light weight aluminum tanks that held 108 gallons of fuel. That extra fuel enabled us to extend our range so that we could protect the bombers all the way to their targets and back home. These external tanks attached one to each wing. After the fuel was expended, the pilot would pull a lever and the tanks would fall to Earth. With the tanks, we could stay in the air for six hours...ooh, that was tough on the ol' bottom! Even today, there is a lot of aluminum scattered throughout Europe. A P-51 carrying drop tanks loaded with fuel would really have its hands full if Luftwaffe fighters attacked. When attacked, we ended up dropping the tanks.

On a long mission it was smart to empty your bladder real good before you went up. We had a tube in our planes. If a fella had an emergency, he could pee in the tube and the urine would flow out the belly of the plane. Look out below! When escorting the heavies, we flew at 20,000 to 35,000 feet. The temperature could be 50-below. Sometimes, flying at high altitude, the tube would not function properly and the pilot could end up with a tube full of pee. The flight leader, seeing his wing man's predicament, might signal the wing man to follow. He would dip a wing, drop a few thousand feet, and then pull back on the stick and make a steep climb back up to altitude. It would be difficult, if not impossible, to keep a lid on that tube. The poor S.O.B. would be soaked in pee. The flight leader would really get a kick out of that. I never had that done to me, and I never did that to anyone else. Some fellas, though, were pretty damned ornery.

On August 28, 1944, we went strafing. First, we hopped over to Bar-le-Duc, France, and topped off our fuel. Our target was Saarbrucken, Germany. On that day we had two aborts. Shortly after we formed up and headed out, Lieutenant McAllister of the 370th Fighter Squadron had his engine seize up and stop running. When the engine stopped, the propeller stopped turning. Better put her down quick before she dropped like a rock. McAllister's plane was now a glider. He had to quickly find a place to put her down, and make a dead-stick landing. He had flap, rudder, and aileron control, but no engine to keep his plane airborne or make corrections. He would get one shot at the landing. He spotted a field. Did he have enough altitude to make it? He turned to the field. Turning slowed the plane down, but meant it lost altitude faster. He didn't want to let the plane slow to stall speed...stall and you spin in. McAllister glided toward the runway. It was too fast, so he pulled up on the stick to slow the plane down. Too slow—nose down and speed picks up but you also lose altitude. By lowering the landing gear, the extra drag slows the plane down and the plane loses altitude, but doesn't stall. A dead-stick landing was tricky business. McAllister made a textbook landing.

We ran into a lot of flak on this mission. Sometimes there was so much flak you wondered how you could fly through it. We did. Sometimes, though, we didn't make it. Lieutenant Suttle was hit by flak. He was unable to bail out and was killed.

Lieutenant Kelsey was my flight leader. I was flying his wing. Lieutenant Gilmore and Second Lieutenant Gordon were also in the flight. The mission at Saarbrucken was to disrupt transportation and troop movement. We were flying at 20,000 feet with clear skies. We had a vivid view of our hunting ground below. Ten miles south of Saarbrucken, we spotted a locomotive with several cars trailing behind.

A train, with steam up, traveling along the countryside could not hide. The rail cars slithering behind it and the smoke pouring from the engine's stack acted like a waving flag to a fighter. A locomotive might get lucky if a fighter had his eye on another target. His only other hope was to get to a tunnel. The locomotive was not lucky on this day.

The engineer saw the glint of the sun reflecting off of the planes. He hoped they were friendlies. The four fighters dipped their wings. "Shit!" he exclaimed. Not what the engineer wanted to see.

The fireman traced the sight line of the engineer up to the diving planes. "Oh, my God," the fireman screamed! As he cried out, tears of realization rolled down his face. The side profiles swung downward and, momentarily, gave the engineer a full top-down view of the diving, turning aircraft. They presented a full frontal view as they continued toward the Earth and the locomotive.

The engineer visualized the route of the tracks that lay ahead. He instinctively pushed the throttle wide open. No tunnels...just rolling countryside ahead. The fighters were at treetop level and closing fast. They looked like angry birds of prey chasing their meal. In an instant, he knew that he could not escape. His body shook, his sweat glands dried in his pale skin. His mind raced. The fireman urinated as he stood frozen, transfixed on the terrifying sight. The engineer grabbed the levers, he cut off the power, and attempted to release steam. He pulled the fireman down to the floor of the cab. He heard the approaching roar of the four fighters. He closed his eyes, cringing, and waited for the terror to erupt. The machine guns exploded to life.

91

Kelsey and I cut loose on the locomotive at a distance of 1,000 feet. Our tracers formed an 'X' that crossed on the locomotive. It blew; smoke and fire shot into the air. We quickly pulled up and turned to avoid flying fragments from the engine. Gilmore and Gordon went after the cars. We made a tight turn and came back around for a second pass. This time, we targeted the cars. We opened up 1,000 feet from the cars. We moved from the front to the back of the train, raking several cars. Gilmore and Gordon followed and nailed more cars. We flew up to 8,000 feet. Below, the locomotive lay shattered and smoldering. The cars lay on their sides in zigzag splintered piles.

Our eyes followed the track west to another locomotive puffing hard to distance itself from the explosions behind it. We came in low and followed the tracks toward the straining engine. We pulled the trigger. The strikes began three cars back from the engine. Pieces of wood, steel, and unidentifiable material leaped into the air. The locomotive flashed bright red and lifted off of the tracks in a violent explosion.

We continued following the tracks westward. We spotted another locomotive pulling six passenger cars. We opened up on the train. No rifles returned fire. Gaping holes ripped open in the tops of the passenger cars. No one could have stuck their head out of windows without losing it. We turned away, perpendicular to the train, then continued around and made another pass. The locomotive belched clouds of steam. Three locomotives destroyed. Parallel to the tracks we spotted trucks and cars on the road. We flew west down the road, opened up on the back of the convoy, and continued firing until we ran out of vehicles. Lt. Kelsey winged over to a field and killed two soldiers who were hiding. I headed down road in the opposite direction and melted an armored car. Kelsey, Gilmore, Gordon, and I regrouped and headed for home.

Saarbrucken was our last mission in August. Flight Surgeon Dunnebier reported that our health was excellent. No new cases of venereal disease. Keep it covered, boys.

In August, 10 men transferred in to the 359th Fighter Group. I became friends with Lieutenant Archibald (we called him Archie) and Lieutenant Leonard Carter. These fellas were placed in my squadron, the 368th Fighter

Squadron. It was natural to make friends with men in your own squadron. We worked, trained, and played together. I had a lot of friends. Archie was a good guy. He was from Connecticut. The 359th Fighter Group had a lot of good men.

Leonard Carter was a good ol' boy from South Carolina. We became good friends. Leonard had a great sense of humor and, according to him, more than one girl was left crying when he shipped overseas. He attended Clemson University, but he wanted to fly, so he left school. He came from a little town called Ehrhardt. He said there were 300 to 400 people in the town. "We all know each other. If you blink, you will miss Ehrhardt." He said there was a little store in town and that's about it. "If you want to go to a real store, you have to drive 45 minutes." Ehrhardt was 70 miles from Savannah, Georgia, and Charleston, South Carolina.

SEPTEMBER, 1944

September 1, 1944, we escort B-17s to Ludwigshafen, Germany. The term that we used when we escorted was "Ramrod," an old term borrowed from the days of the Wild West. A cowboy who herded cattle, rounded up strays, and brought the cattle home safely was called a ramrod. We were the cowboys. We followed our "Big Friends" and made sure they got home safely. If there were any strays (damaged bomber that couldn't keep up with the rest), we would guard/shepherd /protect them until they were safe.

A couple hours into the mission the attack was aborted due to poor visibility. The cloud cover was 10/10 up to 30,000 feet. We turned and headed home. On our return trip, Lieutenant Kaloski developed engine trouble and radioed that he had a runaway prop. A runaway prop was a situation in which the engine revved too high and was out of control. When this happened, the propeller shaft would break or the engine would seize. Kaloski was forced to bail out over the Channel. Lieutenant Boyd was flying Kaloski's wing and called in Kaloski's position. The cloud cover made it impossible for Boyd to spot Kaloski in the water.

The weather improved the next day. Search and rescue found Kaloski's dinghy, but he was not found. A man could not survive long in the water.

Ground crews developed relationships with the pilots. The aircraft were their babies. The crews were bonded to the pilot and the plane. When a pilot was killed, the crew would, at times, gather together and cry as if they had just lost a child.

Two days later, we escorted bombers to Ludwigshafen. Cloud cover was heavy over the target. Bombs were dropped. It could take a few days to know if the target was hit since the results could not be observed from the air.

The fifth of September we returned to Ludwigshafen. Again, results could not be observed due to cloud cover.

Two P-51s from the 368th crashed on take-off. Both pilots escaped unharmed. Two other P-51s from the 368th were hit by flak on the mission. Again, both pilots were unharmed. When flak burst, a red fire ball flashed followed by a black cloud. If the flak exploded close to the plane, the concussion shook the aircraft. A close enough explosion sent shrapnel shooting through the air and pinging off the plane. A closer explosion sent fragments slicing through the skin of the aircraft. We always hoped it would just ping off the plane.

September 8, 1944, we provided escort for B-17s. Take-off went without a hitch. We got in formation and headed out. We made Land-Fall Out (flew over the English Coast). We crossed the Channel and made Land-Fall In (mainland). We flew a tight formation, then my engine started to run rough. I radioed that I was turning back due to engine problem. I turned for home. I made the Channel. I did not want to go down in the Channel. It's not a long flight over the Channel—unless you have engine trouble. Then, it feels like an eternity. Finally, I made it to the coast and then to the field. The engine of my P-51 was inspected...the plugs were fouled.

During September, we were surprised by the return of two of our own. Lieutenant Oliphint, of Bill's Buzz Boys, was reunited with the 359th. He was originally listed KIA and a letter was sent to his mother. After he was shot down, a German patrol checked the crash site. They thought he was dead and left him hanging upside-down in his cockpit. Later, the French Resistance inspected the crash. Also thinking he was dead, they cut his crash straps and he fell to the ground. He let out a moan; he was alive. The Resistance fighters didn't think that they could give him the care he need-ed, so they turned him over to the Germans. The Gestapo got hold of him and gave him enough care to keep him alive, all the while torturing him for information. Eventually, the Germans planned to ship him off to Germany. Oliphint, with help, made his escape. He cut the throat of his Nazi doctor, killed two guards, and met up with the Resistance. Information that he gathered gave Patton valuable intelligence that enabled the U.S. Army to break through the German lines. Oliphint was sent home to convalesce.

Captain Ettleson, also of Bill's Buzz Boys, rejoined the 359th that September, as well. He had worked with the Resistance...until the Allies overran his position. He was transferred back into the 359th and was as-signed to the 368th as squadron leader.

Before daybreak the morning of September 10, 1944, the ground crew was busy preparing the planes for the day's mission. Wheels checked. Marks were made on the tires and wheels. If the marks did not line up, the tire was replaced. Moving parts were checked and lubed, as needed. The engine fluids were checked, the planes were fueled, and the guns were cleaned. The ammo boxes, on the top of the wings, were opened and cleaned. The crew lined up and each person carried a belt of .50-caliber armor-piercing shells. The men took turns handing their belt to the crewman on the wing. The belts were linked together and carefully laid into the box.

A .50-caliber shell was 5.45 inches long...a hardened steel projectile at-tached to a cartridge case that contained a propelling charge. At the back of the cartridge was the primer pocket that housed the primer charge. When the pilot pulled the trigger, the shells were fed to the guns. The firing pin of the gun struck the primer cup/pocket. An explosion occurred and the ar-mor-piercing round (projectile/shell) was expelled from the cartridge. The shell exploded out of the cartridge by a force of 50,000 pounds per square inch. The shell hit its target with devastating consequences. It could tear through concrete or steel. A man would be ripped apart by a .50-caliber shell. Tracer rounds were in each belt. A tracer had a composition behind the projectile that ignited when the shell left the cartridge, leaving behind a trail of fire and smoke. This smoke enabled the pilot to observe the flight of the projectile. The tracer showed the accuracy of his shooting, which was very important. At best, a P-51 could only carry 1,880 rounds, so a pilot had to use his ammo wisely. You would be surprised at how fast 1,880 rounds could be expelled. Guns cleaned, windows polished, checked top to bottom, the plane was mission ready.

This particular day we were escorting B-24s to Stuttgart. After we dropped escort, we did a little strafing. We had strafing maps that identified targets of opportunity, but the Flight Leaders were free to select an area to attack. We searched for targets as we headed west. Below, we spotted a locomotive with several rail cars trailing along. We dipped our wings and picked our targets. Diving on our targets, we chewed up the locomotive and rail cars as if they were toys. It looked like the fourth of July down there as the locomotive belched fire and smoke. The cars splintered as the .50-caliber shells ripped them apart. The cars bounced and twisted themselves into a mangled ruin. Two tracks ran parallel through the countryside; a P-51 targeted the rails themselves. The tracks jumped out of their beds from the .50-caliber strikes. A good day's work.

Meanwhile, the 369th received a "Bandits" call. They engaged the enemy and downed one enemy aircraft and damaged another. The enemy aircraft were Swiss fighter aircraft...not so neutral on that day, I guess.

I did not fly September 12, 1944. Second Lieutenants Haas and Barnett of the 368th did not return from the mission. We weren't sure what happened. All we knew was they didn't come home. Archie crash landed. His plane was totaled, but he was okay. He came up smiling. Lieutenant Carter shot down an FW-190. After he shot down the enemy aircraft, he drew a picture of the action. Leonard was a talented artist. After that, bad weather kept us grounded for a few days.

On September 19th, we provided escort for a mission to Hamm, Germany. Weather over Hamm was 10/10. The B-17s went after secondary targets at Koblenz. They bombed rail targets; three Forts (B-17s) were lost to flak.

B-19 Bomber flying through flak

September 21, 1944, we provided support for the 1st Airborne at Nijmegen, Netherlands. We were to join up with other fighter groups, but the weather turned sour and we were recalled September 22, 1944, we escorted B-17s to Kassel, Germany. Kassel had a tank factory, and the bombers hit their targets. End of tank factory. Three B-17s were downed by flak.

Once again, bad weather grounded us for a couple days, but the ground crew's work continued. Weather did not stop the work in the hangars. Engine overhauls had to be performed. At times, it was decided that it was prudent to replace an engine. Sometimes, when an engine was torn down, the wear on the internal parts was too severe to rebuild. Coolant problems cropped up from time to time. Fuel distribution issues also posed problems occasionally. Issues such as these and others were evaluated and overcome. The crews had to troubleshoot all aircraft that aborted—and prep new planes for action. Planes were readied for the next mission.

September 25, 1944, we were back in the air, escorting B-17s to Frankfurt, Germany. The bombers were after industrial targets. We were in battle formation, trailing the bombers. Near Wiesbaden, flak bursts appeared right behind us, so we took evasive action. We turned sharply and flew to a lower altitude. Second Lieutenant Lauesen was hit by flak and his plane went into a vertical dive. He did not recover the aircraft; we did not see a chute. Two Forts were also downed by flak.

The next day we headed to Osnabrück, Germany. The B-17s hit marshalling yards and a steel mill. We saw a "Big Ben" contrail. When these contrails first appeared, there was a lot of speculation as to what we were seeing.

A contrail was a visible vapor made by the exhaust of the aircraft engines. Hot exhaust gases met cool air and a narrow moist cloud formed in the aircraft's wake. The sighting was called a "Big Ben" because the shape of the distant aircraft looked like London's Big Ben Tower. We later learned that these contrails were from the V-2 Rocket. The Germans had developed the world's first ballistic missile. The V-2 primarily targeted London, England. The Nazis launched 3,000 of these missiles. The rocket carried a warhead that rained destruction on London and killed thousands of people.

This particular day, Pop Doersch flew Lieutenant Beal's plane. Beal's crew chief tucked him in nice and comfortable. Before Pop closed the canopy, the chief handed him a bag. Pop looked at the bag and asked, "What is this?" The chief paused and Doersch looked in the bag. "Rocks! Rocks?" Doersch questioned the crew chief.

"Well, sir, Lieutenant Beal is so bored doing all this escort duty—milk runs, he calls them—that he takes these rocks with him. When he is over the target, he opens his side window and throws rocks at the Germans."

Doersch kept the bag of rocks and when he was over the target, he threw rocks at the Germans.

September 27, 1944, we escorted bombers to Düsseldorf, Germany. On this mission, the bombers were guided to the target by a radar-equipped Pathfinder aircraft. The Pathfinder flew ahead of the main body of bombers and its radar guided it to the target. The plane dropped markers (flares) over the target. The trailing bombers headed for the markers and release their bombs. The use of the Pathfinder greatly improved bombing results.

On the 28th, we escorted bombers to Magdeburg, Germany. The 368th was flying close escort. The heavies hit their target. As they made their turn for home, one B-17 drifted into another B-17's airspace. The two bombers collided violently. Both planes spun in and no chutes came out of either one of them.

Flak was heavy. I could see red flashes from the flak everywhere. After the red flash, the black flak clouds would hang in the air—they filled the sky. Often, anti-aircraft crews would shoot ahead of the planes to gauge range and altitude. The sky would be thick with black clouds and we would think, "We are gonna fly through that? This should be fun." Flak bursts would send shrapnel through the air. A flak burst did not have to hit a fighter to bring it down. A close burst could knock a P-51 out of the air. Sometimes, you could hear "ping, ping, ping" as small pieces hit the aircraft. A direct hit on a bomber's wing would snap the wing right off of the fuselage. A direct hit on the bomber could cause an Earth-shattering explosion and leave a void where the bomber once flew.

On this mission, two bombers received direct hits. There was a sudden explosion followed by a fireball and pieces of airplane arched and spiraled to earth. All said, 23 B-17s were knocked down by flak and by enemy aircraft. Lieutenant Steussy of the 370th was shot down by flak, but was able to bail out. He survived and was taken prisoner.

September 30, 1944, we escorted B-17s to Münster, Germany. All 15 fighter groups of the 8th Air Force were up. The Nazis did not come up to play. Three bombers were knocked down by flak. No fighters were lost.

In September, I was awarded the Air Medal. The citation read, "For exceptional meritorious service in aerial flight over enemy occupied Continental Europe. The courage, coolness, and skill displayed by these officers reflect credit upon themselves and the Armed Forces of The United States." After a pilot earned an Air Medal, he was awarded Oak Leaf Clusters to attach to the Air Medal. I was also awarded an Oak Leaf Cluster in September.

Flight Surgeon Dunnebier reported that our health was excellent. There were no new cases of venereal disease.

OCTOBER, 1944

October 1, 1944, I was promoted to the rank of First Lieutenant, and would now fly as a flight leader. Each flight was made up of four airplanes. There were four flights in a squadron and three squadrons in a group.

October 2, 1944, we escorted B-17s to Kassel. October 3, 1944, we escorted bombers to Nuremberg, Germany. Both missions were routine. No fighters or bombers were lost on either mission.

October 5, 1944, we escorted bombers to Düsseldorf. One B-17 was hit by flak. He was able to fly, so he turned for home. In an emergency, a pilot had to make split-second decisions. This pilot quickly realized he was not in immediate danger. He did not order the crew to bail out. A P-51 stayed to protect him. As he flew over the continent, he continually monitored the flight-worthiness of his aircraft. Look for a place to land, bail out, or continue across the North Sea? The pilot had to constantly evaluate the aircraft's ability to fly. The heavy was losing altitude. Did he have enough altitude? He decided to cross the open water. Halfway to the coast, he realized he was not going to make it. The plane was losing altitude too fast. He ordered the crew to bail out. Nine chutes were seen going into the water. The P-51 radioed the crew's position. Air Sea Rescue got to them in 30 minutes. Only one chute was still on the surface.

On this mission we were flying at 30,000 feet. We were on oxygen. There was a haze at this altitude. Thick cloud tops reached 29,000 feet. Second Lieutenant Bartlett was flying in my element/flight. I observed Bartlett pull way out of formation. I called him on the radio. No answer. He dropped his tanks. I called him again. No answer. The nose of the plane dipped and he entered a tight spiral. I called. No answer. I attempted to follow him through the cloud cover. I lost sight of him. I continued calling Bartlett. No answer. I finally leveled out at 8,000 feet and I radioed in his position. Damn.

October 9, 1944, we escorted bombers to Schweinfurt, Germany. The mission was routine. No bombers or fighters were lost.

October 15, 1944, the target was Cologne, Germany. One B-17 was downed by flak.

October 17, 1944, we again escorted bombers to Cologne. The B-17s were over their target. Bombs were released. A B-17 could carry a maximum payload of 8,000 pounds. Directly over the target there was a violent explosion. A large fireball, a plume of smoke, and pieces of shooting chunks of steel was all there was left of the Fort.

We saw another "Big Ben" that day. The contrail skyrocketed to over 40,000 feet before we lost sight of it.

Lieutenant Anderson was forced to land near Paris. He was there for two days, waiting for his engine to be repaired. When he returned, he had quite a tale to tell. He visited several nightclubs in Paris. The clubs stayed open until 5:00 am. The floor shows featured naked women dancing around the stage. He said they danced with abandon. There were women who would spend time with a soldier for a price. The soldier had to buy a bottle of Champagne and pay a "tip." He said that there were plenty of whores for the Americans. Anderson said that Paris had over 250,000 registered prostitutes. He informed us that these women insisted that a man must wear protection. Prostitutes submitted to required inspections every two weeks. Bordellos were "Off Limits" and were patrolled by MPs. Anderson sure did learn a lot in two days.

October 19, 1944, the target was Ludwigshafen.

October 22, 1944, we escorted bombers to Hanover, Germany. No bombers or fighters were lost on these missions.

We entered the briefing hut on October 24, 1944. Everyone knew it would be another escort. Another Ramrod. There was a lot of excitement when we discovered that we were going strafing. Our destination was south of Hanover. Our job: disrupt transportation. Everyone was pretty wound up. Armed with strafing maps, we took off for Hanover.

On the way in, an element of the 368th engaged two FW-190s. Our fighters quickly shot them down and rejoined the group. They were really excited. Flying escort, we were used to enemy aircraft avoiding contact with us. After flying so many escorts, we were as hungry as a pack of wolves. South of Hanover, we spotted some tasty treats. Two squadrons flew top cover as the third squadron attacked. Then, the attacking squadron rolled up and provided top cover at 8,000 feet. The squadron that was flying cover at 5,000 feet became the attacking squadron. Finally, the third squadron took its turn. Every movement was made with effortless precision. P-51s, three and four at a time, dipped their wings and dove down on targets. We followed the contours of the land, hit our targets, swung around for the next pass, then another, until we handed the baton to the next squadron. Finally, we headed home.

In our rear view we left 27 locomotives destroyed, one locomotive damaged, three flat cars destroyed, 12 trucks, five cars, one goods wagon, and one oil tank car destroyed. Also, 31 flat cars, 18 trucks, 12 goods wagons, and one barge destroyed. The Nazis got a belly full of Mustangs on that day. Three pilots were (forced) to land near Paris because of rough-running engines. Funny how their engines started running rough when they neared Paris!

One of the men (from the 368th) brought back a two-foot section of an ME-109 propeller. We set it in the pilot's lounge in East Wretham. Everyone in the 368th who shot down an e/a signed it.

October 25, 1944, we were back escorting bombers. The target was Reinbek, Germany. We lost one B-17 to flak. No chutes. Ten men died. So far that month, we hadn't lost any bombers to enemy aircraft. We felt pretty damned good about that. We had chased off all German fighters who considered going after our Big Friends. Flak, we had no control over.

Bad weather kept us on the ground several days in October. Winter came early to England in 1944.

October 26, 1944, we escorted bombers to Gelsenkirchen, Germany. The mission was routine. No bombers or fighters were lost.

October 30, 1944, we headed back to Merseburg. The weather was 10/10 all the way to the target. The bombers could not get over the weather (it was cloudy at high altitudes). The B-17s were forced to turn back.

In October, we saw "Big Ben" contrails on almost every mission.

In October, I received my third and fourth Oak Leaf Clusters.

Flight Surgeon Dunnebier reported on the health of the group. No new cases of venereal disease in October. We led all groups (8th Air Force) with the lowest rate of infection. Keep it covered, boys.

NOVEMBER, 1944

The weather in England in November was crappy. It was cold, bleak, and rainy. Crosswinds would blow across the runway, making take-offs and landings a little tricky. Rolling down the runway for take-off, the wind would push us off our center line. When the plane lifted off, the wind would push the aircraft. When landing in a strong crosswind, pilots would make a (crab) landing. The airplane approached the runway, the nose of the plane turned slightly into the wind. The wing was dipped into the wind. In this configuration, the plane tracked on a straight path to the runway. The wind, with the wing dipped, hit the top of the wing. The dipped wing kept the wind from getting under the wing and flipping the aircraft. Just as the pilot was about to touch down, he straightened the nose and brought the wing level, then touched down.

November 4, 1944, Archie had engine trouble and was forced to bail out over Norwich, England. He landed safely and was back at Wretham in time for dinner.

I never wanted to bail out. (Those church steeples are pointy. That would smart.) When a pilot bailed out, it was a last resort. He had to know the plane could not remain airborne and would think, "Do I have enough altitude for my chute to safely carry me to the ground?" He would unbuckle the crash straps. Unlock and open the canopy. Roll the plane to an inverted position and drop out, watching out for the tail section (it would smart if you hit that). Once clear of the plane, he would open the chute and look for a spot to land in a field away from wires, buildings, and other obstacles. Didn't sound like much fun to me.

November 5, 1944, I was flying escort to Frankfurt. We would go strafing after we were released from escort. The weather was so foggy that only 36 of the best pilots were allowed to go up. I was one of the 36. No brag, just fact. When we flew in foggy or cloudy weather, we would fly on instruments. We called it "flying blind." The plane was equipped with a compass, maps, and altimeter. We also knew our air speed. We did not have onboard radar. At the field, the control tower would turn on a beacon and put lights on the runway.

The mission was routine. Soon after we broke escort, we ran into heavy flak and took evasive action. We put the throttles to the wall, then immediately changed course (turned right or left) and changed altitude (higher or lower).

We went hunting after we flew out of the flak. We got 10 locomotives. We lit them up. We destroyed box cars, trucks, and a bus full of soldiers.

This is a good time to tell you about an incident. I'm not saying on which mission the incident occurred. We were strafing. There were troops in trucks or rail cars. One pilot did not open fire on the troops. After we returned to the field, I quietly took the pilot aside and asked him why he didn't open fire. He told me that he just couldn't shoot. He said that the soldiers were helpless and couldn't defend themselves...it was like shooting fish in a barrel. I told him that those "helpless" soldiers were headed to the front. They were about to do everything in their power to kill Americans. It was our job to inflict as much damage on the enemy as we possibly could. "Next time, you will pull the trigger. Next time, you will engage the enemy and inflict as much damage upon them as you can." He apologized and said that he would. I told him not to apologize, "Just do your job."

Lieutenant Haines was hit by small-arms fire while strafing. One bullet in the coolant system would bring down a P-51. He crash landed and was taken prisoner. Captain Brown also crash landed. He was behind Allied lines when he crashed. He was unhurt.

November 6, 1944, we escorted bombers to Hamburg, Germany. Four B-17s were downed by flak; 40 men dead. No fighters lost.

November 8, 1944, we escorted B-17s to Merseburg. Three bombers were lost to flak. One of them went down in flames in the middle of Frankfurt. We saw four chutes.

After we were released, we went strafing. Major Howard of the 369th Fighter Squadron was hit by 20-mm shells. His P-51 began smoking. He was unable to maintain control of the plane. The fighter went into a spiral. The plane exploded when it went in.

November 9, 1944, we escorted bombers to Metz. Colonel Tacon led

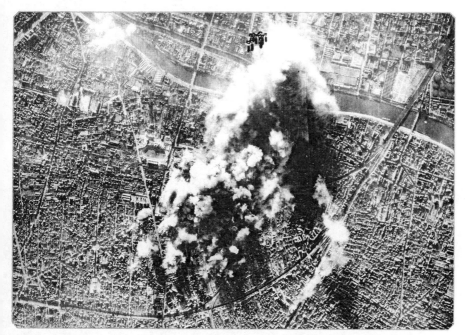

Bombs dropped on target. Photograph made from B-17 Flying Fortress

the group. This would be his last flight with the 359th. The colonel had led the 359th since it was created. Brigadier General Anderson, commanding general of the 67th Fighter Wing, selected Tacon to become his chief of staff. Lieutenant Colonel Randolf would assume command of the 359th Fighter Group.

The mission was routine. No bombers or fighters were lost.

The weather was so bad that we did not fly any missions from the 11th through the 19th.

November 20, 1944, Lt. Col. Randolf led the mission. We escorted bombers to Bonn, Germany. On our return home, Lieutenant Barth developed engine trouble and was forced to bail out over the English Channel. That time of year a pilot could only survive for about eight minutes in the water. Air Sea Rescue spotted an oil slick in the water and found his overturned dingy. Lt. Barth was not found.

November 21, 1944, we escorted bombers to Merseburg. The target: synthetic oil facilities. The bombers were flying at 24,000 feet. Elements of the 370th and 369th Fighter Squadrons were flying top cover at 31,000 feet. The 368th Fighter Squadron and elements of the 370th Fighter Squadron were flying close support. The 359th Fighter Group put up 55 P-51s. We were also joined by the 352nd Fighter Group. Our strength was 100 P-51s.

We rendezvoused with the bombers over Hasselt, Belgium. One hour after rendezvous (r/v), the call "Bandits" went out over the radio. Top cover spotted 135 enemy aircraft. Within 30 minutes of the initial contact, another 200 were spotted. The enemy was not eager to engage us. They wanted the bombers. They probed here and there. They would have to engage us. The fight was on. The sky was clear at 24,000 feet. Clouds were above us, so we did not have visual contact with the top cover. We maintained close support and could hear the action over our radios. Fighters came after the bombers. We interceded as much as we could. Every time we went after an attacking fighter, he would dive down on the deck. We maintained close support. If they drew us away from the bombers, the enemy would decimate the vulnerable B-17s. The fighting (and chasing off) lasted an hour. We fought the enemy fighters as we approached the target, flew over the target, and exited the target. Six B-17s were shot down.

Ten-thousand feet above us, the battle raged on. Over the radio we heard, "He's on your six, break right, I got him, two on your tail," and so on. We could see the results of the fight above us. Airplane parts began falling through the bomber formations. Fireballs that were planes streaked to Earth. Pilots floated down through our formations, parachutes on fire. Burning men tumbled to Earth. The conclusions of battles that went badly for losers rained down all around.

Captain Ray Wetmore of the 370th Fighter Squadron was flying close support. He was the leading ace of the 359th Fighter Group. We called him "laser eyes" because he could spot e/a at 60 miles. All of us flying close support wanted to join the fight above. We also knew we had to maintain close support. Wetmore began screaming into the radio, "Send down a live one! Send down a live one! To hell with that, all that's coming down are burning airplanes and parachutes! Send me a live one!" He sure was a character.

That day, the 359th and 352nd shot down 17 enemy aircraft, had two probables, and damaged seven. Three P-51s did not return from the battle. Lieutenant Anderson was shot down and taken prisoner. Lieutenants Stegmerski and McGeever were shot down and killed.

November 25, 1944, we again went to Merseburg. I stepped outside for that first cigarette. I watched the bombers heading out. When we flew to Merseburg, I would log about five-and-a-half hours. A B-17 would log between nine-and-three-quarters and 10 hours. That was one long day for our Big Friends.

The flak that day was the heaviest any of us had ever seen. The air was so thick with black clouds, a person could walk on it. We were hoping that we would get another shot at their fighters. Maybe they didn't like the results of our last tango. As heavy as the flak was, no B-17s were lost to flak. No P-51s were lost to flak. I guess the Nazis forgot their glasses that morning.

November 27, 1944, I did not fly. The 359th went on a strafing mission and encountered heavy flak over Germany. They split up into flights and were scattered across Germany. Captain Wetmore was flying with his wingman, Lieutenant Robert York. Wetmore spotted a hundred ME-109s and a hundred FW-190s. Wetmore called in his position to any flights of the 359th that might be in the area. He and York shadowed the enemy aircraft. They were behind and at 6:00 high. Wetmore called again for assistance. He said, "Come on and hurry up. If you don't get here soon, York and I are gonna have to shoot them all down by ourselves."

It turned out they couldn't wait any longer. The two were spotted by the Germans, who began peeling off in flights of four to attack the P-51s. Wetmore hollered to York, "You take the one hundred on the right and I'll take the one hundred on the left." The fight lasted 25 minutes. When the smoke cleared, six German fighters were shot down. York scored three kills and Wetmore scored three kills. Wetmore's plane was damaged, but he and York returned safely to East Wretham.

As Wetmore and York headed for the clouds and homeward, Blue Flight of the 370th joined the fight. Lieutenant Dick Connelly and his wingman, Lieutenant "Windy" Windniller, made their attack from an altitude of 34,000 feet. They dove on the ME-109s. Windy got one immediately and turned on a second fighter. He nailed the second enemy aircraft and sent it down in flames. Windy then heard Connelly over the radio, "The son-of-a-bitch has shot me down. I'm bailing out." Elements of the 369th and the 368th joined the fight and downed five more enemy aircraft.

This was Connelly's last mission. He was scheduled to head back to the States. He had had a premonition that he would be shot down on the last mission of his tour. Connelly went down with his plane and was killed on the last mission of his tour.

Flight Surgeon Dunnebier reported on the health of the 359th for the month of November. Our record of no venereal disease came to an end in November. He reported that there were two cases of gonorrhea and two cases of syphilis. As a result of these cases of venereal disease, all enlisted and ground officers would have to attend one-hour lectures every Friday evening until headquarters advised otherwise.

I received one Oak Leaf Cluster in November.

DECEMBER, 1944

December 1, 1944, was a damp, dreary day. No flying that day.

December 5, 1944, we escorted bombers to Berlin, Germany. Flak was very heavy over the target. Nine bombers were lost and 105 were damaged. No P-51s were lost.

Morale was high for the Allies. There was a lot of talk about the war coming to an end. Many thought the war would be over by Christmas. Ground forces were running through the enemy lines—destination: Berlin. From the air, we were crippling the enemy's industry, transportation, and their ability to wage war. Christmas did not seem an unrealistic date.

December 6, 1944, we again went to Merseburg. The target was the synthetic oil industry. Flak was intense. Enemy fighters were a no show. No fighters or bombers were lost.

Merseburg was an important target. Knock out the Nazi oil industry and planes couldn't fly, tanks couldn't fight, and trucks couldn't carry troops into battle.

Billy D. with his P-51K, Richie 1st, named after his brother Richard Kasper

December 11, 1944, we escorted B-17s to Frankfurt. The target: marshalling yards. December 12, 1944, we escorted B-17s to Merseburg.

December 16, 1944, the Nazis mounted a massive counter offensive that would be known as The Battle of the Bulge. The weather was so poor that no planes could get up to engage the enemy. The Germans cut through our lines and forced the Allies to retreat. Thousands of Americans were killed as a result of this offensive. The Germans ran low on fuel, the weather cleared, and bombers pounded Nazi positions. The fighting would not, however, be over by Christmas.

I did not fly on December 18, 1944. Two of my friends, Lieutenants Archibald and Olsen, did not return from their mission that day. We found out much later what happened to them. The two engaged several enemy aircraft. Between them, they shot down nine e/a before they were shot down. Both men became aces that day. Archie was seriously injured when he crashed. He would need two canes to walk when he was well enough to move. Olsen was also injured when he was shot down. Archie and Olsen would spend the rest of the war in a POW camp.

December 24, 1944, we escorted bombers to Hartenrod, Germany. The target was the airfield at Hartenrod. We encountered flak. Two B-17s were hit by flak and exploded. On the way out, we encountered enemy fighters. Lieutenant Boyd got tangled up with three e/a, and his plane was severely damaged. He was forced to bail out and was taken prisoner.

We had a Christmas Eve service. Lieutenant Colonel Randolf opened the service by lighting a candle for our friends who had lost their lives. I sent my brother, Richard, a Christmas present. It was a picture of me with my plane. The name of the plane was "Richie 1st."

Bad weather grounded us Christmas Day. We had 200 orphans on base and fed them turkey, pork, steak, and more. It was quite a spread. We also handed out gifts to the kids.

December 26, 1944, we escorted B-24s to Koblenz. The target: a marshalling yard and a bridge. The weather was so bad that only volunteers flew. Fifty-five of us went on the mission. No planes were lost.

December 27, 1944, we escorted bombers to Kaiserslautern, Germany. No planes were lost.

December 28, 1944, we flew to Siegburg, Germany. The 368th flew ahead of the bombers. As we approached the target, we dropped chaff—streamers of aluminum that blinds enemy radar. It must have worked because no bombers or fighters were lost.

December 30, 1944, we escorted B-17s to Limburg, Germany. One bomber was downed by flak.

December 31, 1944, we escorted bombers to Misburg, Germany, and an aircraft factory at nearby Wenzendorf. The 368th Fighter Squadron was flying close support. Near the target, ME-262s (jets) made a run at the bombers. We moved between the jets and the bombers. We got off a couple short bursts, and the jets turned away to avoid us. FW-190s then came at the bombers. We again got between them and the bombers. We repeated this little dance several time with the FW-190s and the ME-262s.

Four B-17s were shot down by FW-190s. Flying close escort, the P-51s were spread out over a lot of sky. We did our best to engage and turn away would-be attackers, but we were not always successful. Top cover was able to engage several enemy aircraft. Unfortunately, we couldn't save them all. One bomber, hit by flak, exploded over the target. Twelve e/a were shot down. We lost Lieutenant Murphy from the 368th. Pilots from his element were engaging e/a. When they regrouped, he was nowhere to be found. We have no idea what happened to him.

In December, I earned one Oak Leaf Cluster.

Flight Surgeon Dunnebier reported two new cases of venereal disease. The venereal disease lectures would continue. Now the chaplain was called in to educate the boys. He presented the church's view on promiscuous sexual relations. Keep it covered, boys.

JANUARY, 1945

January 1, 1945, we furnished escort (ramrod) support for bombers. The target was Magdeburg. I was an acting group leader. We rendezvoused with the bombers near Ratzeburg, Germany, at 1145. I heard a report of "Bandits!" I took my group up to meet the threat. We went up to 32,000 feet to look for the e/a. At 1150, I got bounced by a ME-109 and took evasive action. He didn't get any good strikes on my plane, but the maneuver I made to avoid his attack stalled my engine at high altitudes. Especially in the winter, our canopies could ice up...mine did. (Probably iced when I yelled, "Shit!")

I cleared my canopy and put the nose down to recover from the stall. I spotted the ME-109. Three P-51s were trying to get on his tail. He was banking left and performing a Luftberry, which was a tight circle in an attempt to circle behind attacking enemy fighters. Nothing beat a Luftberry like a tighter Luftberry—and that's what I did. I cut inside his circle and at 25 yards and a 30-degree angle of attack, I pulled the trigger. The hits started forward of the cockpit and continued under and behind his cockpit. As I was shooting, pieces of airplane began flying as the plane disintegrated. The ME-109 caught fire. It began to tumble and the pilot bailed out. An aerial kill. "Hot damn!" I told my flight, "Keep your eyes peeled for any more bandits." I got one! This one didn't run like so many others; he was aggressive. Wetmore and York also got one each, Carter damaged one, and Adkins finished it off. The Nazis still had plenty of fight in them.

Shoveling snow and chipping ice off of runway

When I got home, I signed that propeller in the 368th's hall. The signed propeller is on display at the Mighty 8th Air Force Museum in Savannah, Georgia.

I was coming to the end of my tour. I sat down with Lieutenant Colonel Randolf, who informed me that a discrepancy in my combat hours had been discovered. I had been writing down less time than I was actually in the air. I wanted to keep flying combat missions. I was doing what I had dreamed of since I was a small boy. I knew my flying days would end, but I wanted it to last as long as possible. The colonel said that he understood why I had shorted my hours. He appreciated my wanting to stay with it, but he said, "We need to give the boys coming up a chance to get in the fight." He said that I could fly four more missions. First, though, I was to take leave and go to a rest home.

Pilots usually are scheduled to go to a rest home about halfway through their tour. Rest homes were scattered throughout England, and were places where pilots and bomber crews could spend a week or two to relax and get away from combat. I had put it off. I wanted to keep flying. But I had my orders, so I went to the rest home, where I met some other pilots and bomber crews. When the bomber crews found out that I was a Little Friend, they all wanted to shake my hand and thank me. I accepted the thanks, but didn't want to make too big of a deal about it. So, I relaxed with them and drank warm English beer.

While I was gone, Lieutenant Beaupre of the 368th crashed and died on take-off. That winter was one of the worst in recorded history. Ground crews were kept busy shoveling snow and chipping ice off of the pierce plank runway. When that runway had snow or ice on it, it was like a skating rink—the slickest surface I had ever been on.

January 13, 1945, Captain Shearer of the 369th crashed eight miles north of the field after take-off. He was killed instantly.

January 14, 1945, I was not scheduled to fly. The 359th escorted bombers to Hemmingstedt, Germany. After the target was hit, our fighters were released from escort and went after targets of opportunity. A flight led by Captain "Pop" Doersch spotted e/a near an airfield. The Germans had 20-mm ack-ack to protect the field. Doersch and his wingman, Lieutenant Jack McCoskey, ignored the 20-mm guns and went after FW-190s. Doersch quickly shot one down, then he and McCoskey went after another FW-190 from different angles of attack. The FW-190 applied full flaps and Doersch overshot him. The maneuver also worked on McCoskey as he went in for the attack. When McCoskey overshot, the e/a, his fighter stalled. The P-51 inverted and slammed into the ground at 400 miles per hour. It exploded as a result of the violent crash.

Pop and McCoskey were good friends, and Doersch was enraged at what he had just seen. He re-engaged the FW-190 and raked the German plane with his .50-caliber machine guns. The enemy aircraft went down in pieces. The pilot bailed out. Doersch was still seething. He made a pass at the German's billowing chute in an attempt to collapse it. He failed. He gathered his emotions and did not make another pass at the pilot. Unlike McCoskey, the German would live to fly another day.

January 15, 1945, we escorted bombers to Lechfeld, Germany. The mission was routine. No fighters or bombers were lost. It was good to be up in the air again.

January 16, 1945, we escorted B-24s to Ruhland, Germany. The target was the synthetic oil industry. Lieutenant Colonel Randolf led the group. I was flight commander for the 368th. One by one, we took off and circled while the group joined up. Second Lieutenant McLean made a run at take-off. He aborted his first attempt. He taxied back around and made a second run at take-off. On his second attempt, he crashed. His plane had a full load of fuel and the P-51 exploded into a large fire ball. McLean was a good kid. He may have had engine trouble—don't know. There is a marker for him at a nearby cemetery.

We headed out toward Ruhland. At 1100 hours, Lieutenant Lupton, also in my flight, had an oil-pressure problem and was forced to bail out over the Netherlands. He landed safely, but we found out later that he was killed. I don't know the details, but he was killed. If the Gestapo got their hands on a pilot, there was a good chance the pilot would be murdered. I don't know if the Gestapo was involved.

We didn't encounter the Luftwaffe that day. Flak was heavy. Two B-24s were downed by flak. On our return trip we were ordered to land on the continent; East Wretham was closed because of bad weather. We returned to the field the next day.

January 28, 1945, we escorted B-17s to Cologne. The target was marshalling yards. We had seven aborts...the winter was tough on man and machine. Flak was heavy. One Fort exploded over the target; three others were downed by flak. On this mission, 172 bombers were damaged by flak.

I didn't fly on the 29th. My squadron lost a pilot that day. Lieutenant Daniels inadvertently strafed an American installation northwest of Strasbourg. He made three passes. On the second pass the Americans gave him a warning burst from a machine gun position. When he made his third pass, they shot him down. He died in the crash.

In January, the 359th lost five pilots in flying accidents.

In January, I received two Oak Leaf Clusters.

No venereal disease reported during the month, so the lecture series was discontinued. Maybe they should have gotten the chaplain involved sooner.

The winter was cold, snowy, and just plain nasty. Because of the poor weather, everyone was put on Sulfadiazine to prevent respiratory disease.

We also got a prisoner of war report from the Red Cross. One of the new prisoners was McCoskey. When we heard the news, we were all stunned—especially Pop Doersch. None of us could understand how McCoskey could have survived such a horrific crash. He went in inverted at 400 miles per hour and the plane exploded. There was no chute. We were told that when the plane exploded, somehow the explosion threw McCoskey clear of his P-51. His only injury was a badly broken jaw...a miracle in anyone's book.

Pop said, "It's a good thing I didn't kill that German when he parachuted. If I had, they would have killed Jack for sure."

FEBRUARY, 1945

In February, I was promoted to captain. One more mission and I was done. I was not career military. It was near the end my tour. I had no college. Despite these factors, my commanding officers promoted me. I was proud that they recognized my hard work and my leadership skills.

February 5, 1945, we escorted bombers to Wenzendorf, Germany. The weather was crappy. I got into line to take off. The engine sounded great—purring like a kitten. It was my turn. I gave it some throttle. The steel pierce plank runway was slick. I rolled right down the center of the runway. Faster and faster I rolled. Sometimes, on nasty days, I could almost hear Frank, "Faster, Billy! Faster!" I made take-off speed and she lifted up into the gray sky. We headed out in tight formation. No accidents on take-off. We were up for 45 minutes and then we were recalled. The weather was too bad to complete the mission. We would try again the next day.

February 6, 1945, we headed to Wenzendorf. No recall. We rendezvoused with B-17s over the continent. Flak was heavy at the target. Three Forts were downed by flak. Ten other shot-up Forts made it home, but they were so badly damaged that they never flew again.

After the mission, I met with the colonel. I had flown my last mission. Randolf asked me if I had given any thought to staying in the Air Corps. I told him that I didn't have any college, so I thought my options would be limited. He asked if I had considered being an instructor. The Air Corps would need good instructors who had combat experience. I told him that being a flight instructor was more dangerous than fighting the Nazis. When I was behind the stick I had control, and that was the way I liked it. He laughed and said, "Okay, then...not an instructor." I told the colonel that I thought I would use my G.I. Bill to go to college. After that, I would look at my options. He thought that was a good plan. Then, he told me that I was not scheduled to ship back to the States yet, and he gave me leave to go to London.

The next day, I packed a bag and headed out. I got a jeep ride to the train station in Thetford. I boarded the train and was off to London. It was a cold ride. There were heat levers over the seats. I reached up and turned the heat on; it didn't work. I tried another—same result. As it turned out, none of those heat levers worked. The windows on the train were iced up. I rubbed a spyhole on the glass. Through it I saw leafless trees, smoke from homes rising and blending into the bleak, gray sky, and stone fence rows peeking out of their snowy hiding places.

The train jerked to its scheduled 20-minute stop in Ely, then resumed and pulled out of Ely Station. Along the way, it would slow and move to side tracks, yielding to speeding freight trains. The train snaked its way across the countryside. Finally, London was in sight. The skyline had been altered by tons of bombs and thousands of ballistic missile strikes. Amazingly, London's most famous buildings remained standing. Somehow, six years of war had spared these familiar sights. London was a large, sprawling city. One quarter of the houses in the city had been destroyed, and thousands of civilians had been killed. The train squealed to a stop in the station. I grabbed my bag and headed out. I saw piles of rubble where buildings once stood, but people on the street went about their day as if all was normal.

I settled into a room and did some sightseeing. In and around the destruction I saw untouched buildings rising above the piles of rubble. A tall building stood seemingly untouched. All around it were piles of rubble where neighboring buildings once stood. The city was still alive and strangely beautiful standing in the middle of twisted, heaping piles of yesterday's air raid results. Big Ben, Buckingham Palace, Westminster Abby, and other landmarks seemed to ignore the war. The city was like a prizefighter. It took blow after blow, bloodied and bruised, and remained standing.

In London, a pilot had an advantage over the other fellas with the ladies. The wings on my collar drew the women like a magnet. Two bars on my uniform didn't hurt, either. A fella could get used to that kind of attention. Hmmm. A career in the Air Corps...we'll see.

One day I was walking the streets, searching for a nightclub. As I made my way down a street, I saw a familiar face. It couldn't be. I quickened my pace to get a closer look. It was him! It sure as hell was! It was Aspane! My tormentor! Would I lose my bars? Would I put lumps on him? I got to within two feet of him. He faced me. His questioning look turned to recognition. He gave me a weak smile and his gaze fell to the ground. I took in this picture. The cocky look of superiority was gone. A look of shame filled his face. In front of me stood the man who had taken so much pleasure in making me miserable. Shoulders hunched and head hung, his voice meekly greeted me. There was no power, no life in it. He wore Second Lieutenant bars. Second Lieutenant? He came over more than a month before me. I could never be a politician. I cut the crap and got to the point. "Aspane, why are you still a Second Lieutenant?" My brain went from battle stations to "at ease."

His gaze dropped again. He said that he had flown 20 missions. "I can't go up again." His eyes had the look. He told me that he knew that if he went on another mission, he wouldn't come home. "I would be killed," he said. He was sure that his number was up. I recognized the look in his eyes. In two minutes I had gone from wanting to put lumps on the guy to... "Aww, shit." It was called a self-fulfilling prophesy. A fella thought his number was up and it was up.

I put my arm around his shoulders and said, "Come on, I'll buy you a drink."

That was the last time I saw Aspane. We had a drink together and a couple of laughs. After that, I went on my way. There was no shame in what happened to Aspane. He was not a bad person, he was not a coward. He was a casualty...the same as if he had been shot. A young man going to war was like going in for a complicated surgery. You didn't want to know all the details, and you prayed that you didn't wake up on the table. Aspane woke up.

The train ride back to Thetford was just as cold and jerky as the ride to London. When I returned to East Wretham, I thought I would get my orders home. Instead, I was briefed on events that occurred while I was on leave.

February 7, 1945, Lieutenant Thompson (368th) bailed out and landed in the North Sea. Search and rescue did not find any trace of him.

February 9, 1945, Captain Ettleson (368th squadron commander) was doing a little strafing. He was last seen strafing a locomotive. The cause of his crash was unknown. The last of "Bill's Buzz Boys" was gone.

Lieutenant Colonel Evans (Headquarters) and Lieutenant Garrett (368th) were taken prisoner February 14, 1945.

Lieutenant Maiorano (368th) was forced to bail out over the continent when his engine overheated. He was in the process of making his way back to England.

In short, the 368th was short-handed. I was granted an extension. I got to take "Richie 1st" up for one more ride. One thing I had learned was to live in the moment. Enjoy each day. Don't make a lot of plans. It was easy for me to get back in the cockpit. As a matter of fact, I was happy to go up again. Flying the P-51 was an opportunity to ride the tiger one more time. I had absolutely no apprehension.

February 19, 1945, we escorted B-17s to Dortmund, Germany. The target was an oil refinery. Lt. Maiorano made his way back to us and was flying a replacement P-51. We rendezvoused with the bombers at 1320, and were flying at an altitude of 25,000 feet. We spread out and flew in their bomber stream, which was the white vapor created by the hot engine exhaust when it met the cold air at high altitudes. The four engine bombers each created four trailing vapor clouds. We danced in and out of the vapor streams as we trailed our Big Friends.

Prior to reaching the target, I led the 368th ahead of the bombers. We dropped chaff and the aluminum streamers floated to earth. The chaff confused the enemy radar. The anti-aircraft guns would fire blindly without the radar. Flak was heavy over the target. The radar could have gotten a bead on us before we dropped chaff. Flak appeared around us. Ping, ping, ping, ping. Pieces of shrapnel hit my plane. I quickly checked my instruments. All normal. No visual damage. No smoke or fluids appeared. "Let's get the hell out of the target area," I radioed. We took evasive action, and the flights peeled off left and right. We escaped the flak blasts. No bombers were lost. The chaff worked.

On the way out, Maiorano radioed that his coolant had popped. "You've got to be kidding me! Two missions in a row!" I thought. He called that he was bailing out. We were near Trier, Germany. A pilot in his flight yelled, "He's standing up in his cockpit!" He didn't roll over and drop out. As he lifted his leg to step out of the cockpit, the wind hit him full in the chest and blew him backward. He fell into the tail section of his plane and was lodged there for a few seconds. His plane was descending into the cloud cover below. His body rolled off the tail section and fell through the clouds. The plane then disappeared into the clouds. His flight leader reported that he did not see a chute.

We headed home. I waited for my orders, but instead received one more extension. Yes, I got to take "Richie 1st" up again. This was definitely my last mission. I had orders sending me Stateside. This would also be Lieutenant Leonard Carter's last mission—my friend from South Carolina.

I woke up early February 25, 1945. I looked out the window. The sky was clear. I splashed my face with water, got dressed, and ran a comb through my hair. I smoked a Chesterfield and headed to breakfast. After I ate, I enjoyed another smoke with a cup of coffee. I had a few laughs with Carter and some of the other guys.

I made a pit stop and headed for the waiting trucks. I unloaded and walked into the briefing room. "Stormy" gave us the weather report. I focused on the map. The target was the marshalling yards at Munich. The bombers were already on their way out, with Colonel Randolf leading. The briefing ended and we walked outside for the chaplain's prayer.

After the prayer, we headed to the pilot's shack. I stepped into my flying suit, and grabbed my Mae West and helmet. I made my way to S-2 (Intelligence). I flashed my dog tags and handed over my wallet. Nothing else was in my pockets. I shoved the escape kit into one pocket, the course card and map into another pocket, and headed toward "Richie 1st." Doersom was waiting for me, just like he had 69 times before. I handed him my helmet and we shared a smile. "I don't think they are gonna let you go home, sir. They like you so much they're gonna keep you here."

"That would be okay with me, Chuck," I said as I handed him my helmet. "How's she running today?"

"Like a kitten, Bill. Purring like a kitten."

I climbed the wing and said, "Let's make her roar like a lion."

Doersom tucked me into the cockpit, like a mother tucking her child into bed. I fastened the crash straps. Radio plugged in and turned on. Gyro compass and altimeter set. Gun and pitot heat on. Ship's clock set to correct time. Brakes on and flap switch up. Doersom slid the bubble-top canopy forward.

"Chocks out!" I yelled.

"Clear."

I turned on the battery and the ignition switch. Fuel pump and gas line on. I primed the engine and hit the starter button. She whistled and sputtered and stopped. It was cold out. She needed a little more loving before coming to life. I hit the primer again and then the starter.

She sputtered and shook and reluctantly came to life. Within seconds, she was running smooth. All 12 cylinders were firing in perfect timing. I could feel her power in my hands. I could hear her power. She was a beautiful beast. I was going to open the door to her cage and free her.

Doersom and I shared our love of engines. An engine man used all of his senses. Sight, sound, touch, and smell. Engine men were like musicians who created a masterpiece. We were a part of our creation. We were artists immersed in our artwork. Yes, I am still talking about an engine.

For a moment, I thought about home. I was fortunate to be able to share this bond with Frank. Engines completely changed the dynamic of our relationship. We could take cold pieces of steel, put them together, tune them, turn a switch, and bring the thing to life.

Flaps came up. I looked down at Doersom and he saluted. I returned his salute. Hell, he never saluted. I smiled and nodded to him. I gave her some throttle and taxied into position. Instruments looked good. I revved her up and she said, "Let's go."

I rolled to take-off position and gave her the throttle. She rolled faster and faster down the runway. Take-off! I never grew tired of take-off. That moment when I broke gravity's hold. Come to think of it, I think I always had a smile on my face when I would lift off the ground. When a fighter took off, it ripped itself free of the ground and leapt into the air. I was soaring with the eagles. The feeling was almost indescribable. WOW!

I climbed and got into position. We circled until everyone was up, then headed out in formation. I heard two aborts over the radio. We flew over the English countryside. Instruments looked good. She sounded good. Out over the water. We approached the continent. Over land. We rendezvoused with the heavies over Strasbourg, France, at 1030.

Battle formation. We spread out in the B-17s bomber streams. We neared the target and the flak appeared. A B-17 exploded over the target. The sky shook. Another one was hit and caught fire. Nine chutes came out of the burning Fort.

Bombs away at 1128. The target took some good hits. We could see several fires below. We turned for home and crossed the continent. English Channel ahead. Engine instruments and fuel looked good. We flew over the North Sea...England was dead ahead.

East Wretham came into view. We circled. It was my turn, so I lined up the runway. Wheels down. "Richie 1st" glided smoothly over the runway. I feathered my landing and we touched ever so gently. I taxied to my parking spot. That was it. I was done.

I turned in my equipment and got my wallet, jacket, and cap. Leonard ran over and clowned around with me. He was quite a character. He handed a camera to another pilot and hammed it up as we got our picture taken. As he laid his head on my shoulder and did his best Laurel and Hardy imitation, I told him, "Just don't drool on my shoulder, Leonard!"

"Make sure we get a good picture of those bars on him," Leonard joked with our cameraman.

Like my hours, I didn't write everything down in "The Pilot's Diary." I understand that there was a fire that destroyed a lot of records. None of that really mattered. I was just happy I got to live a dream. Maybe someday the Air Corps will release my gun camera footage.

We received word from the Red Cross that Lieutenant Maiorano was alive and he was a prisoner of war. That lucky Italian lived! What do you know?

I received an Oak Leaf Custer in February. I had one Air Medal with eight Oak Leaf Clusters. I flew 70 missions and logged 323 combat hours.

Some historians would write that the 359th Fighter Group was a "Colorless Unit." I beg to differ. The men I fought with did everything their country asked of them. They were no better or no worse than any other unit that served their country. So, to those who would call us a "Colorless Unit," I say, "Phooey"—and you can quote me on that. How can someone say that my friends who fought and died were "colorless?" Shame on them.

The 8th Air Force suffered more than 20,000 killed and tens of thousands injured. Thousands more were taken prisoner. I don't know why so many had to die. I still believe in God, but know He doesn't owe me an explanation. If He feels it necessary, maybe someday He will let me know. In my youth I had even considered entering the ministry, however after my war experiences I knew that wasn't the path I would follow.

The 359th Fighter Group flew combat missions in Europe from December 13, 1943, until April 25, 1945. The 359th was active for 17 months. During that time period, 372 men flew combat missions and 78 pilots were killed. Thirty-five men were taken prisoner. I was one of the lucky ones. (You were right, Ma I was always coming home.)

My Uncle, Raymond Bailey, had spent his tour in the war in field hospitals and had seen his share of death and destruction. Raymond worked as an orderly in the hospital. He also drove an ambulance. Field hospitals were located as near the front as possible. The Army placed these hospitals there so that a wounded soldier could receive treatment as soon as possible. The safety of the medical staff and the patients was also considered when setting up a hospital. The hospital was set up far enough from the front so that it, hopefully, wouldn't come under enemy fire.

"We've got a pilot." The word went out as an injured pilot was brought in for treatment. As soon as he could, my uncle Raymond would make his way to the pilot. Whenever a pilot was brought in, he would rush to see if it was his nephew, Billy. If the pilot was not Billy, then "Billy must be all right," Raymond thought.

Raymond knew I was in Europe during the war, but he didn't know any more than that. My exact whereabouts had been classified. He would nervously approach an injured pilot. I guess in his mind, I was okay as long as he didn't see me lying on a stretcher in his hospital.

One-hundred and twenty-five of our planes were destroyed and 228 aircraft were damaged. The men of the 359th shot down 356 enemy aircraft and destroyed 121 on the ground. We destroyed 335 locomotives and damaged another 147. We destroyed 337 railroad cars and damaged 1,119. The 359th destroyed 144 motor vehicles, as well as buildings, railroad tracks, communication towers, power transmission facilities, boats, barges, and more. Not bad for a "colorless" Fighter Group.

Leonard and I traveled to Liverpool together. We talked about our time in East Wretham, and toasted our friends who would never come home. Leonard told me that he was going back to Clemson University.

Leonard and I boarded the Queen Elizabeth for our return trip home. It was a crying shame the way that beautiful ship had been vandalized. Handrails had been carved up with knives, graffiti scribbled on the walls, furniture broken, and more. I was raised to respect other peoples' property. I guess some people weren't.

The ship docked back in the U.S.A. Leonard and I headed for the train station. He boarded one headed for Ehrhardt, South Carolina, and I headed to Springfield, Ohio.

I was given a two-week leave. It had been over a year since I had seen my family...it seemed like a lifetime. The train went to Springfield via Chicago. I had a five-hour layover in Chicago. Some of the family came to the train station to see me. I picked up Shirley May to bring her to Springfield to stay with Frank and Thelma. She sure was excited about the train ride. Sometimes the simplest things in life are the best. Nighttime on the train rolled around. The porter changed our seats into a bed and then pulled down the top bunk and made it up. Shirley May exclaimed, "I want to sleep on the top bunk! I want to sleep on the top bunk!"

"Okay, Shirley May," I said as I gave her a boost up. Then, it was lights out. I was just getting close to dozing off when I heard, "I don't like the top bunk! Can I have the bottom bunk? Billy, can I have the bottom bunk?"

"Yes, Shirley May. You can have the bottom bunk."

The top bunk of a sleeper is real cozy. As I found out, a man my size didn't have much room to maneuver. After banging my head a couple times on the ceiling, I finally found a comfortable position and drifted off to sleep. Life was good.

The train pulled into Springfield, Ohio. Frank, Ma, Richie, and Grandma Bailey were there to greet us. I smiled ear to ear. It was good to be home. I stepped off the train and was greeted by hugs and wet kisses. Richie was bouncing up and down. "I showed everybody at school the picture of you and my plane!" I sure got a big kick out of that. The next day, I went to the shop and talked to the fellas at work. I visited with friends and relaxed at home.

I told Frank and Ma that I wanted to go to college when I got out of the service. The G.I. Bill would pay for my school and books, but I would need money for expenses because I didn't think that I could work and go to school. I asked them if they could help me out. They said that they were sorry, but they didn't have the money to give. I understood. I never again asked for money.

After my leave, I headed out to Santa Ana, California. My new post was the Army Air Corps Redistribution Station Number Four. I was not called to fight in the Pacific Theater. I remained at the Redistribution Station until I was transferred to Lubbock, Texas. I needed some transportation, so I bought a car. I also bought a nice pair of Lucchese cowboy boots. I really liked those boots.

While in Texas, I logged 34 hours in the AT-6. June 26, 1945, I was transferred to Victoria, Texas. On July 25, 1945, I was discharged. I weighed 189 pounds when the Air Corp gave me my last physical. That was the last time I would see the 180s.

THE MEN WHO FLEW...

Addleman, Robert H., 1st Lt., South Bend, Indiana. **CT**

Adkins, Boyd N., Jr., 1st Lt., Stiltner, West Virginia. **CT**

Alexander, Robert S., F/O, Brooklyn, New York. **OD**

Allen, John C., 2nd Lt., Prichard, Alabama. **KIA**

Albertson, Benjamin H., Capt., San Antonio, Texas. **PW**

Ambrose, Vincent W., Capt., Baltimore, Maryland. **CT**

PILOT'S STATUS	
CT	Completed Tour.
KIA	Killed in Action.
KNO	Killed on Training Mission.
TRFD	Transferred.
PW	Prisoner of War.
I	Interned in Neutral Country.
OD	On duty 1 September, 1945.

Anderson, Carl M., 2nd Lt., Boston, Massachusetts. **KIA**

Archibald, David B., 1st Lt., Suffield, Connecticut. **PW**

Ashenmacher, Joseph M., 1st Lt., Hartford, Wisconsin. **CT**

Aunspaugh, Merle G., 2nd Lt., Gothenburg, Nebraska. **KNO**

Baccus, Donald A., Lt.-Col., Los Angeles, California. **OD**

Bach, Glenn C., Capt., Olympia, Washington. **CT**

Baker, George F., Jr., Capt., Fulton, New York. **CT**

Baker, Wilson K., Jr., 1st Lt., Atlanta, Georgia. **I** (Sweden)

Baldridge, Arlen R., 1st Lt., Poca, West Virginia. **KIA**

Barber, Kenneth E., 1st Lt., Turner, Oregon. **OD**

Barnett, Louis E., 2nd Lt., Detroit, Michigan. **KIA**

Barth, Merle B., 1st Lt., San Leandro, California. **KIA**

Barlett, Clifford L., 2nd Lt., Manchester, New Hampshire. **KIA**

Bateman, Jack H., 1st Lt., McIntosh, Florida. **TRFD**

Bateman, Paul H., 1st Lt., Rockingham, North Carolina. **CT**

Beal, Elby J., Capt., Angelton, Texas. **CT**

Bearden, Lawrence A., 2nd Lt., Greensboro, North Carolina. **KNO**

Beaupre, Robert V., 1st Lt., North Attleboro, Massachusetts. **KIA**

Becker, Claire A., 2nd Lt., Moline, Illinois. **OD**

Bell, Gwyn W., 2nd Lt., St. George, South Carolina. **OD**

Bell, John E., 2nd Lt., Louisville, Kentucky. **OD**

Bellante, Emidio L., 2nd Lt., Easton, Pennsylvania. **TRFD**

Benefiel, Robert E., Capt., Walla Walla, Washington. **CT**

Benneyworth, Albert F., 2nd Lt., Nashville, Tennessee. **OD**

Berndt, Harley E., F|O, Wansan, Wisconsin. **TRFD**

127

Blackburn, George H., Jr., 2nd Lt.,
Abilene, Texas. **KIA**

Bolefahr, Wayne N., Capt.,
Grosse Point, Michigan. **KIA**

Booth, Robert J., 1st Lt.,
Waukeska, Wisconsin. **PW**

Borg, Robert M., 1st Lt.,
Chicago, Illinois. **CT**

Botsford, Raymond L., 1st Lt.,
Puyallup, Washington. **KNO**

Bouchard, Lawrence W., 1st Lt.,
Ogdensburg, New York. **TRFD**

Boussu, Marvin F., Capt.,
Frederick, South Dakota. **OD**

Boyd, Ray A., Jr., 1st Lt.,
Oak Ridge, Louisiana. **PW**

Braymen, Kenneth M., 2nd Lt.,
Shenandoah, Iowa. **OD**

Breuning, Charles R., F/O.,
San Antonio, Texas. **KIA**

Brickner, Albert C., 2nd Lt,
York, Pennsylvania. **OD**

Brinkmeyer, Jack W., 2nd Lt.,
Cairo, Illinois. **OD**

Britton, Eugene F., 1st Lt.
Mansfield, Massachusetts. **CT**

Broach, Richard H., Capt.,
Otisville, New York. **PW**

Brown, Carey H., Capt.,
Kingsport, Tennessee. **KNO**

Brown, Clarence R., 2nd Lt.,
Aberdeen, Mississippi. **OD**

Brown, Grover W., 1st Lt.,
Hickory Grove, South Carolina **OD**

Brown, Ralph L., 2nd Lt.,
Richmond, Virginia. **CT**

Brown, Wayne W., Major.
Neillsville, Wisconsin. **KNO**

Brundae, Lowell W., 1st Lt.,
Spokane, Washington. **KIA**

Buchanan, William E., 1st Lt.,
Royal Oak, Michigan. **CT**

Buckley, James E., Capt.,
Philadelphia, Pennsylvania. **KIA**

Buniowski, John F., Capt.,
San Pedro, California. **CT**

Bur, Thomas G., 2nd Lt.,
Green Bay, Wisconsin. **TRFD**

129

Burgsteiner, Will D., Capt.,
Voldasta, Georgia. **CT**

Burt, Harold R., 2nd Lt.,
Bremerton, Washington. **KIA**

Burtner, Rene L., Jr., 2nd Lt.,
Washington, D.C.
MIA-EVADED-OD

Burton, Herbert C., Capt.,
Crawfordsville, Indiana. **TRFD**

Burton, Robert E., 1st Lt.,
Wilmar, California. **CT**

Byron, George J., 2nd Lt.,
Waterbury, Connecticut. **OD**

Cald, Vernor L., 1st Lt.,
Detroit, Michigan. **CT**

Callahan, Robert M., Capt.,
Cleveland Heights, Ohio. **CT**

Campbell, Robert W., 1st Lt.,
Syracuse, New York. **CT**

Cannon, Donald E., 1st Lt.,
Hebron, Nebraska. **CT**

Carroll, Walter J., 1st Lt.,
Teaneck, New Jersey. **OD**

Carter, Clifford E., 1st Lt.,
Los Angeles.
KIA

Carter, Leonard D., 1st Lt., Ehrhardt, South Carolina. **CT**

Carter, Richard G., 2nd Lt., West Newton, Massachusetts. **OD**

Cater, Emer H., 1st Lt., Manchester, New Hampshire. **KIA**

Cavanaugh, Cornelius J., 1st Lt., Royal Oak, Michigan. **CT**

Chaffee, Vernon E., F/O., Waycross, Georgia. **TRFD**

Chatfield, Donald W., 1st Lt., Waycross, Georgia. **CT**

Cherry, Willis J., 2nd Lt., Cleveland Heights, Ohio. **PW**

Cimino, William L., 2nd Lt., Houston, Pennsylvania. **OD**

Clark, Buell R., 2nd Lt., Winchester, Indiana. **OD**

Clark, Edward L., 2nd Lt., West Allenhurst, New Jersey. **OD**

Collins, Cornelius J., 1st Lt., Binghampton, New York. **TRFD**

Collins, John F., Jr., Capt., Hartford, Connecticut. **TRFD**

131

Collins, William F., Capt. Jonesville, Wisconsin. **OD**

Connelly, Dick D., 1st Lt., Pensacola, Florida. **KIA**

Cook, Emory C., 1st Lt., Waterford, Connecticut. **CT**

Cooley, John D., Jr., 1st Lt., Aberdeen, Maryland. **OD**

Cosmos, Alexander M., 1st Lt., Antioch California. **KNO**

Cowie, Albert A., 2nd Lt., Glendale, California. **KIA**

Cox, Ralph L., Major, Psadena, California. **OD**

Crane, Lewis G., Capt., Auburn, New York. **CT**

Cranfill, Niven K., Lt.-Col. Temple, Texas. **CT**

Crawford, Cecil W., 1st Lt. Demopolis, Alabama.

Crenshaw, Claude G., Capt. Monroe, Louisiana. **KIA**

Cunningham, Charles V., Capt., Revere, Massachusetts. **CT**

Cuzner, Harry F., 1st Lt.,
Chicigao, Illinois.   **CT**

Daniels, Richard H., 1st Lt.,
Ticonderoga, New York.   **KIA**

Dauohert, Eugnee F., 2nd Lt.,
Appleton Wisconsin.   **TRFD**

Davison, Robert W., Capt.,
Roselle, New Jersey.   **CT**

Deen, Grover C., 2nd Lt.,
Austin, Texas.   **PW**

Denman, John A., Capt.,
Houston, Texas.   **OD**

Doersch, George A., Major,
Seymour, Wisconsin.   **OD**

Downing, John L., 1st Lt.,
Atmore, Alabama.   **CT**

Drake, Olin P., 1st Lt.,
Palisades Park, New Jersey
TRFD

Dunlap, Elmer N., 2nd Lt.,
Victoria, Texas.   **PW**

Dunmire, Daivd P., 1st Lt.,
Niagara Falls, New York.   **KIA**

Enoch, Clifton Jr., 2nd Lt.,
Princeton, Kentucky.   **KIA**

133

Eliott, Robert H., 1st Lt.,
Forest City, North Carolina. **OD**

Erwin, Robert D. 1st Lt.,
Woodward, Oklahoma. **OD**

Ettlesen, Charles C. E., Capt.,
Summit, New Jersey. **KIA**

Evans, Roy C., Lt.-Col.,
San Bernardino, California.
TRFD

Everhart, Olin C., 2nd Lt.,
Wenatchee, Washington. **TRFD**

Ferris, James J. III, 1st Lt.,
Englewood, New Jersey. **KNO**

Flack, Jack O., 1st Lt.,
Palmetto, Florida. **CT**

Fladmark, Osca R., Capt.,
Sioux Falls, South Dakota. **CT**

Fogg, Howard L., Capt.,
Summit, New Jersey. **CT**

Fong, Frank S., 1st Lt.,
Miami, Florida. **TRFD**

Ford, Marlyn C., 1st Lt.,
Jacksonville, Florida. **OD**

Forehand, William C., Major,
Kokoma, Indiana. **CT**

Foster, William B., Jr., 2nd Lt.,
Pittsburgh, Pennsylvania. **TRFD**

Francis, Robert. M, Capt.,
Chicago, Illinois. **OD**

Fraser, Lewis L., 1st Lt.,
Lakeland, Florida. **TRFD**

Freeman, Albert S., 1st Lt.,
Hendersonville, North Carolina.
OD

Gaines, Robert S., Jur., Capt.,
Edgerton, Wisconsin. **CT**

Garrett, Roy C., 2nd Lt.,
Tallahassee, Florida. **KIA**

Garth, Horace E. III, 1st Lt.,
Huntsville, Alabama. **TRFD**

Gates, Harold R., 1st Lt.,
Binghampton, New York. **TRFD**

Giese, Arthur J., Jr., 1st Lt.,
Detroit, Michigan. **TRFD**

Gilmore, Chester R., Capt.,
Medway, Massachusetts. **CT**

Givan, George M ., 2nd Lt.,
Milwaukee, Wisconsin.

Gordon, John T., 1st Lt.,
KIA

Gray, Rockford V., Major,
Dallas, Texas.
TRFD—KIA (9th AF)

Grimes, Howard E., 1st Lt.,
Bedford, Massachusetts. **KIA**

Gugemos, Robert J., 1st Lt.,
Lansing, Michigan. **OD**

Haas, James H., 2nd Lt.,
Phillips, Wisconsin. **PW**

Hagan, Benjamin M. III, 1st Lt.,
Chattanooga, Tennessee. **PW**

Haines, Maurice N., 2nd Lt.,
Camden, New Jersey. **PW**

Hair, Lynn W., 1st Lt.,
Dallas, Texas. **KIA**

Hanzalik, Frank, 1st Lt.,
Chicago, Illinois. **CT**

Hastings, Willia., m-H1st Lt.,
Texarkana, Texas. **CT**

Hatter, Robert B., Capt.,
Ottawa, Illinois. **CT**

Hawkinson, Robert W., Capt.,
Chicago, Illinois. **PW**

Heim, William J., 1st Lt.,
Oakland, California. **OD**

Herb, John W., 2nd Lt.,
University Heights, Ohio. **KIA**

Hess, Le Roy D., 2nd Lt.,
Tulsa, Oklahoma. **PW**

Highfield, Jack D., F/O,
Greenville, Michigan. **TRFD**

Hill, Joseph M., Jr., F/O,
Logansport, Indiana. **OD**

Hipsher, Charles W., Capt.,
Allendale, Illinois. **CT**

Hobson, Kenneth L., 2nd Lt.,
Birch Run, Michigan. **PW**

Hodges, Fred S., Major,
Memphis, Tennessee. **OD**

Hodges, William R., Capt.,
Winston-Salem, North Carolina.
MIA-EVADED-CT

Holliday, Frank W., 2nd Lt.,
McCook, Nebraska.
KIA

Hollis, Harold D., 1st Lt.,
Holton, Kansas.
KIA

Hollomon, Ivan B., 1st Lt.,
Newport News.
MIA-EVADED-OD

Homeyer, Albert G. Capt.
Burton, Texas. **CT**

137

Hopkins, Robert W., Capt.,
Leesburg, Virginia. **OD**

Hovden, Lester W., 2nd Lt.,
Ridgeway, Iowa. **KIA**

Howard, James A., Major,
Minot, North Dakota.
KIA

Hruby, Conrad Z., F/O.,
Sloan, New York.
OD

Hudelson, Clyde M., Jr., 1st Lt.,
Modesto California. **KIA**

Hughes, John E., 2nd Lt.,
Mobile, Alabama.
KIA

Hunter, John B., Capt.,
Mansfield, Ohio. **CT**

Huskins, Sam J., Jr., Capt.,
Burnsville, North Carolina. **CT**

Hutton, James F., 2nd Lt.,
Jones, Michigan. **IA**

Hylland Edward J., 2nd Lt.,
Philadelph,ia, Pennsylvania. **KIA**

Irvine, Chaunney S., Major
San Francisco, California. **CT**

Janney, Raymond B. II, Capt.,
Norristown, Pennsylvania. **CT**

Jenner, Russell H., 2nd Lt., Lakewood, Ohio. **KIA**

Jennings, Warner C., 1st Lt., Benton Harbor, Michigan. **OD**

Johnson, Emory G., 1st Lt., Centre, Alabama. **CT**

Jones, Cyril W., Jr., 1st Lt., Athens, Tennessee. **KIA**

Judkins, Vernon T., 1st Lt., Prosser, Washington. **OD**

Kaloski, Edward G., 2nd Lt., Long Island, New York. **TRFD**

Kasper, Billy D., Capt., Springfield, Ohio. **CT**

Keesey, John S., Capt., Pine Grove, Pennsylvania. **CT**

Kelly, Dale E., 1st Lt., Centuria, Wisconsin. **OD**

Kelly, John H. III, 1st Lt., Lyons, Colorado. **OD**

Kelsey, Joseph P., Capt., Cincinatti, Ohio. **CT**

Kerns, John E., 2nd Lt., Sol Pasadena, California. **KIA**

139

Keur, John E., 1st Lt.,
Chicago, Illinois. **CT**

Kibler, Ralph E., Jr., 1st Lt.,
Morganton, North Carolina. **KIA**

King, Benjamin H., Major,
Oklahoma City, Oklahoma. **CT**

King, Herman E. 2nd Lt.
TRFD

Kirk, Karl H., Capt.,
Warren, Ohio. **TRFD**

Klaver, Ralph R., 1st Lt.,
Palmyra, New York. **OD**

Klem, Thomas J., 1st Lt.,
Glen Lyon, Pennsylvania. **TRFD**

Klock, Richard E., F/O,
Binghampton, New York. **OD**

Klug, John H., Jr., F/O,
Chicago, Illinois. **KNO**

Koenig, Harold E., F/O,
Akron, Ohio. **OD**

Kosc, George J., 1st Lt.,
Long Island, New York. **CT**

Kreuzman, Henry B., 1st Lt.,
Cincinatti, Ohio. **OD**

Kruger, Charles H., Capt.,
Willoughby, Ohio. **CT**

Kysely, Arvy F., 1st Lt.,
Knowlton, Wisconsin. **CT**

Laing, D. H., 2nd Lt.,
Montgomery, Alabama. **PW**

Lambright, Clarence M., Capt.,
Houston, Texas. **CT**

Lamont, John W., 1st Lt.,
Seattle, Washington. **CT**

Lancaster, Raymond B., Capt.,
Galveston Texas l(Sweden)

Lancaster, Robert T., 1st Lt.,
Bangor, Maine. **OD**

Lane, Thomas S., Capt.
Lockport, Illinois. **CT**

Lanier, John T., F/O,
Forest City, Arkansas. **OD**

Lauesen, John F., 2nd Lt.,
Chicago, Illinois. **KIA**

Leathley, Eric H., F/O,
Detroit, Michigan. **TRFD**

Lemmens, Andrew T., Major,
Canandaigua, New York. **OD**

Levitt, Leon J., 2nd Lt., Villa Ridge, Illinois. **TRFD**

Lewis, Wilbur H., Capt., Long Branch, New Jersey. **CT**

Linderer, Howard A., 1st Lt., Enid, Oklahoma. **KIA**

Lindsey, Douglas G., 1st Lt., Alexandria, Virginia. **OD**

Long, George W., 1st Lt., Mason County, West Virginia **OD**

Lovett, James K., Major, Red Bay, Alabama. **CT**

Lubien, James J., 2nd Lt., Berwyn, Illinois. **TRFD**

Lupton, Graham, 2nd Lt., Mount Pleasant, South Carolina. **KIA**

Lux, Frank O., Capt., Albany, New York. **CT**

Lyon, Washington D., Capt., Durham, North Carolina. **KIA**

MaGee, Raymond E., Capt., Mulberry, Kansas. **CT**

Maclean, Douglas A., 2nd Lt., Iron Mountain, Michigan. **KIA**

Madison, Garland E., 1st Lt., Gadsden, Alabama. **OD**

Maiorano, Anthony D., 2nd Lt., Detroit, Michigan. **PW**

Major, Ross O., 1st Lt., Chicago, Illinois. **TRFD**

Marcinkiewicz, John S., 2nd Lt., Bondsville, Massachusetts. **PW**

Marr, John M., 2nd Lt., Columbus, Indiana. **TRFD**

Marron, John T., 1st Lt., Crawfordsville, Indiana. **OD**

Marshall, Frank R., Jr., Capt. Burlington, Kansas. **CT**

Marshall, William J., 1st Lt., Philadelphia, Pennsylvania. **OD**

Marson, Alfred D., 1st Lt., Pittsburgh, Pennsylvania. **TRFD**

Martin, Allan G., 1st Lt., Detroit, Michigan. **OD**

Martin, James C., 2nd Lt., Atlanta, Georgia. **OD**

Maslow, Edward J., 1st Lt., Plymouth, Pennsylvania. **PW**

Mason, Robert G., F/O, Jacksonville, Florida. **OD**

Matthew, Harry L., Capt., Wilsonburg, West Virginia. **CT**

McAlevey, John F., 1st Lt., Brooklyn, New York. **CT**

McAlister, John W., Jr., 1st Lt., Greensboro, North Carolina. **TRFD**

McCluskey, Paul E., 2nd Lt., Edgerton, Kansas. **KIA**

McCormack, James W., 1st Lt., New York City, New York **KIA**

McCormack, Robert E., 1st Lt., Oswego, New York. **OD**

McCoskey, Jack E., 1st Lt., Mishawaka, Indiana. **PW**

McDonald, James H., 1st Lt., St. Pauls, North Carolina. **OD**

McGeever, Thomas J., Capt., Birmingham, Alabama. **KIA**

McGehee, Fred S., 1st Lt., Marianna, Florida. **OD**

McGregor, Garland J., 2nd Lt., Greenville, South Carolina. **KIA**

McInnes, Robert L., Capt.,
Massillon, Ohio. **CT**

McIntosh, Robert W., 1st Lt.,
Jackson, Michigan. **OD**

McKee, Daniel D., Lt.-Col.,
Greenville, Mississippi. **OD**

McNeill, John W., Jr., Capt.,
Red Springs, North Carolina. **CT**

Mejaski, Joseph W., Capt.,
Tucson, Arizona. **CT**

Melrose, Don S., 1st Lt.,
Kirkwood, Missouri. **KIA**

Merry, Milton S., Capt.,
Detroit, Michigan. **CT**

Mettel, Arnold F., 1st Lt.,
Aurora, Illinois. **CT**

Meyer, Lawrence F., 2nd Lt.,
Apalachicola, Florida. **KIA**

Miller, George D., 1st Lt.,
Fountain City, Tennessee. **OD**

Millis, Tracy E., 1st Lt.,
Saratoga Springs, New York. **OD**

Minchew, Leslie D., Capt.,
Miami, Florida. **OD**

145

Montague, Bert M., 1st Lt., Raleigh, North Carolina. **OD**

Morrill, Myron C., Jr., 2nd Lt., South Plainfield, New Jersey. **KIA**

Morris, Arthur B., Jr., 1st Lt., Cordele, Georgia. **OD**

Morris, Thomas W., 1st Lt., Miami Beach, Florida. **OD**

Mosse, Charles W., Capt., Phœnix, Arizona. **PW**

Murphy, Donald L., 1st Lt., Grand Blanc, Michigan. **KIA**

Murphy, John B., Lt.-Col., Darlington, South Carolina. **CT**

Murray, John J., 1st Lt., Cooper Plains, New York. **OD**

Murray, Wallace C., 2nd Lt., Phœnix, Arizona. **IA**

Muzzy, Raymond G., F/O, Milwaukee, Wisconsin. **OD**

Newberg, Warren R., 1st Lt., Brockton, Massachusetts. **CT**

Newcomer, Earle S., 1st Lt., Reading, Pennsylvania. **TRFD**

146

Newton, Madison H., 1st Lt.,
Anton, Texas. **OD**

Niccolai, Albert T., 1st Lt.,
Kenosha, Wisconsin. **KIA**

Oakley, Robert G., 1st Lt.,
Lakewood, Ohio. **CT**

Oliphint, John H., Capt.,
Shreveport, Louisiana.
PW—Escaped

Olson, Paul E., 1st Lt.,
McKeesport, Pennsylvania. **PW**

Orwig, Eugene R., Jr., Capt.,
Los Angeles, California. **CT**

O'Shea, James H., 1st Lt.,
New York City, New York. **CT**

O'Shea, James J., F/O,
Lynn, Massachusetts. **KIA**

Page, Donald G., 1st Lt.,
Taft, California. **OD**

Painter, Jefferson C., 1st Lt.,
Spartanburg, South Carolina.
TRFD

Parsons, James R., Jr., 1st Lt.
Norfolk Virginia.
KIA

Parsons, James W., Lt.-Col.,
North Hollywood, California.
OD

Patton, Lee, 1st Lt.,
Winnetka, Illinois. **OD**

Perrin, Grant M., Capt.,
Geneva, Ohio. **CT**

Perkins, Earl P., Capt.,
Frederick, Oklahoma. **CT**

Pezda, Edwin F., Major,
Hamtramck, Michigan. **PW**

Pherson, Robert L., Capt.,
Volant, Pennsylvania. **KIA**

Pino, James R., 1st Lt.,
Whittier, California. **PW**

Porter, Alan C., 2nd Lt.,
Greenwood, Delaware. **KIA**

Porter, Roger W., 1st Lt.,
Brockton, Massachusetts. **CT**

Prewitt, Luster H., 1st Lt.,
Malaga, New Mexico. **CT**

Rabb, Richard, O 2nd Lt.,
Augusta, Georgia. **I** (Sweden)

Ralston, Gilbert R., Jr., Capt.,
Buechel, Kentucky. **CT**

Ramser, Galen E., Capt.,
Elyria, Ohio. **CT**

Randolph, Gaston M., 1st Lt.,
Asheville, North Carolina. **CT**

Randolph, John P., Col.,
Sckertz, Texas **CT**

Rea, Frank Jr., 2nd Lt.,
Detroit, Michigan. **OD**

Reese, Luther C., F/O,
Brunswick, Georgia. **KIA**

Rodeheaver, Homer L., 1st Lt.,
Jellico, Tennessee. **KIA**

Ruggles, James J., 1st Lt.,
Flushing, New York. **OD**

Rueschenberg, Werner J., 1st Lt.,
Westphalia, New York. **CT**

Sackett, Stanley E., 1st Lt.,
Fort Collins, Colorado. **KIA**

Sander, Robert B., 2nd Lt.,
Newton, Massachusetts. **KIA**

Sansing, Virgal E., 1st Lt.,
Lexington, Massachusetts.
TRFD

Scheeter, Harry L., 2nd Lt.,
Bronx, New York. **TRFD**

Schulte, Jack R., 2nd Lt.,
McDonald, Ohio. **TRFD**

Schwartz, Benjamin D., 1st Lt.,
Pittsburgh, Pennsylvania. **OD**

Seller, Wilbur W., Jr., Capt.,
Terre Haute, Indiana. **OD**

Semple, Harry D., 2nd Lt.,
Meadsville, Pennsylvania. **TRFD**

Shaw, Clifton, Major,
Gainesville, Texas. **CT**

Shearer, Karl K., Capt.,
Vandalia, Ohio. **KIA**

Shoffit, Jimmy C., Capt.,
Ft. Worth, Texas. **CT**

Shortness, Gordon M., 2nd Lt.,
Dearborn, Michigan. **KIA**

Shouse, Russell E., 1st Lt.,
Jasonville, Indiana. **OD**

Shupe, Joseph E., 2nd Lt.,
Bristol, Tennesse.e **KIA**

Siltamaki, Robert W., 1st Lt.,
Hanna, Wyoming. **PW**

Simmons, William R., 1st Lt.,
Norfolk, Virginia. **KIA**

Sjoblad, Edwin L., 2nd Lt.,
Chicago, Illinois. **KIA**

Smith, Alma R., 1st Lt.,
Salt Lake City, Utah. **CT**

Smith, James B., 1st Lt.,
Georgia. **PW**

Smith, Samuel R., Capt.,
Wichita Falls, Texas. **TRFD**

Smith, Seymour, 2nd Lt.,
New York City, New York.
TRFD

Smith, Thomas P., Capt.,
Moodus, Connecticut.
PW--Escaped--OD

Soderman, Byron N., 1st Lt.,
El Campo, Texas. **OD**

Staley, Charles W., 1st Lt.,
Brooklyn, Wisconsin. **TRFD**

Stanley, C. L. 1st Lt.,
Parks, Texas.
TRFD

Staup, Homer A., Capt.,
Dayton, Ohio. **TRFD**

Stegnerski, Stanley F., 2nd Lt.,
Chester, Pennsylvania. **KIA**

Stepp, William F., Capt.,
Allison Park, Pennsylvania. **OD**

Steussey, Howard E., 2nd Lt.,
Port Arthur, Texas. **KIA**

151

Stevens, Jack D., Capt., Inglewood, California. **CT**

Straub, Richard P., 1st Lt., Erie, Pennsylvania. **OD**

Stubblefield, Charles E., 2nd Lt., Whittier. California. **KIA**

Sundheim, Paul E., 2nd Lt., Buffalo, New York. **KIA**

Surowiec, Eugene L., Capt., Albertson, Pennsylvania. **OD**

Suttle, Ferris C., 2nd Lt., Lancaster, South Carolina. **KIA**

Sutton, Thomas C., Capt., Santa Ana, California. **OD**

Swanson, William H., Lt.-Col., Chicago, Illinois. **CT**

Tacon, Avelin P., Col., Shreveport, Louisiana. **CT**

Taylor, Lester G., Jr., Capt., Kansas, Missouri. **CT**

Tenenbaum, Harold, 1st Lt., Detroit, Michigan. **OD**

Thacker, Robert L., Capt., Sioux City, Iowa. **CT**

Thomas, Earl W., Jr., 2nd Lt.,
Binghampton, New York. **KIA**

Thomas, Wendel G., 1st Lt.,
San Antonio, Texas **TRFD**

Thompson, Henry L., 2nd Lt.,
Tyler, Texas. **KNO**

Thomson, Bryce H., 1st Lt.,
Flint, Michigan. **TRFD**

Thomson, Robert C., Major,
Bellmore, New York. **CT**

Thorne, Edward J., 1st Lt.,
Swisvale, Pennsylvania. **PW**

Tilton, Elbert W., 1st Lt.,
St. David, Arizona. **CT**

Tuchscherer, Daniel R., 1st Lt.,
Menasha, Wisconsin. **CT**

Tucker, William N., Jr., 1st Lt.,
Hertford, North Carolina. **KIA**

Turinsky, George 1st Lt.,
Luzerne, Pennsylvania. **TRFD**

Tyrrell, Albert R., Lt.-Col.,
Fresno, California. **PW**

Vos, Benjamin J., Jr., 1st Lt.,
Lafayette, Louisiana. **KIA**

153

Way, James L., Jr., Capt., Lincoln, Nebraska. **OD**

Welch, Edward L., 1st Lt. Dallas, Texas. **CT**

Westall, Frank E., Jr., 2nd Lt., Columbia, Ohio. **KIA**

Wetmore, Ray S., Major, Kerman, California. **OD**

White, Bennie F., 2nd Lt., Alexandria, Louisiana. **KIA**

White, Samuel A., Jr., 1st Lt., Hammond, Louisiana. **CT**

Wiley, Walter W., F/O, Washington, Pennsylvania. **PW**

Wilson, James V., Lt.-Col., Elwood City, Pennsylvania. **PW**

Wilson, John W., 1st Lt., Trenton, New Jersey. **CT**

Williams, Harvey C., 1st Lt., New Freedom, Pennsylvania. **TRFD**

Williams, Theophalus A., 1st Lt., Sonora, Texas. **KIA**

Windmiller, Donald L., Capt., Slater, Mississippi. **OD**

Wolfe, Albert E., Capt.,
Nanticoke, Pennsylvania. **CT**

York, Robert M., Capt.,
Old Orchard Beach, Maine. **CT**

Zizka, Lawrence A., 1st Lt.,
Howell, Michigan. **KNO**

Image Courtesy U.S. Air Force

The P-51 Mustang, a long-range single-seat fighter aircraft,
was the first fighter that could escort bombers deep into enemy territory.
The P-51 became one of WWII's most successful and recognizable aircraft.

AFTER THE WAR:
LONG STORY SHORT

ONWARD TO CIVILIAN LIFE

Transitioning from military life and the war to life as a civilian again proved easier than I imagined. I went back to work at National Supply. The company needed people to go into the field and install and repair engines, so I interviewed and was selected. Installations and repairs took me all over the western United States, as well as to Canada, Mexico, and South America. I spent a lot of time in Venezuela—there was a lot of work there—and I learned enough Spanish to get around, order meals, and carry on simple conversations. I traveled for about three years before deciding that it was time to stay and work in Springfield.

I flew a few times out of the Urbana and Springfield Airports. I flew a PT-19 and an Ercoupe. The top speed for these planes was 132 miles per hour—that's a long way from 400-plus in a P-51. Flying can get pretty expensive. That was one good reason that I only flew six times after the war. Frank and Rich wanted me to take them up in an airplane, so out to the Springfield Airport we went. I took them for one hell of a ride...as good as the PT-19 could give. Rich was yelling, "Please!" and "Billy, please! I want to land!" I think Rich got religion that day.

When we touched down, Frank scrambled out of the plane and puked. The airport manager approached me, wide eyed. He said that he was sorry, but he couldn't let me take that plane up again. I thanked the fella. Frank, Rich, and I headed home. You can take the pilot out of the fighter, but you can't get the fighter out of the pilot. All fighter pilots think that they can drive as good as A.J. Foyt—they can't.

Billy D. in 1948 at age 25

I hadn't been home long when Grandma Bailey died in February 1948. Raymond and Shirley May came to Springfield for the funeral. Later that year, in November, I lost my other grandmother. Grandma Kasper had moved in with Uncle Dick and his family after Grandpa died in 1931. She helped out in Uncle Dick's grocery, making donuts. Several years after Grandpa died, she developed breast cancer but refused to see a doctor. After she endured a long and painful period of suffering, we lost her. Grandma Kasper was the last of that generation, which started me thinking more about my future and the possibility of finding a girl and settling down.

Meanwhile, Frank and Thelma were still renting on West Southern Avenue in Springfield, but they wanted to move out of the city. Frank wanted a garden. The problem was, they couldn't come up with the down payment. I told them that I wanted to help. I would use my G.I. Bill and get a V.A. loan, so that's what we did. I bought a two-story house that was on one and two-tenths acres. The property was located in Beatty Town on Route 68, three miles south of Springfield. Later, I would transfer the deed into my parents' names.

The house needed a lot of work. The back of the house needed to be shored up. We tore down and rebuilt walls and put in new floor boards. We rebuilt the bathroom. Richard was old enough to help and he pitched in, volunteering to paint the bedrooms. I set him up with paint, brush, roller, pan, and drop cloths. He poured paint in the tray and soaked the roller in it (and I *do* mean he soaked the roller). He swung that roller toward the wall and—ZIP—a rooster tail of paint sprayed the ceiling, floor, Richard, and me (on the other side of the room). Some paint actually went on the wall. As he turned around and faced me, he was spitting paint. I said, "Close your mouth when you are painting. Well, Rich, you are off to a fast start. Try a little less paint and roll slower." I wiped paint from my shirt. We painted inside and out. The house also needed caulking around windows and doors. Outside, we put up a three-rail wood fence and fixed up the single-car garage.

House on S Yellow Springs Pike, Route 68, where Thelma and Frank Kasper lived from 1948-1970

It was a nice house when we were finished. The front door opened to an enclosed porch. There was a large living room with wood flooring. On the north wall was a working fireplace. At the southwest end of the room, stairs climbed to the bedrooms. Moving west through the living room and past the stairs was the dining room. The dining room table and hutch were on the left. Stairs that led to the cellar were at the southeast corner of the room. To the right, between two straight-back chairs, sat an end table. Beyond the dining room was a rectangular-shaped kitchen. At the back of the house was an enclosed porch and the bathroom. The floor ran downhill and to the right as you walked across the enclosure to the bathroom, but the floor was level enough.

It was around that time that I met George Gibson at a bar. He became a great friend, and he and I ran around a bit. Sometimes, James Kirkendall, an Ohio State Highway Patrolman, would run with us.

One day, George and I went to the State Theater to see a movie. Before the movie, they ran some newsreels. On the big screen appeared a clip from a fighter's gun camera. I knew that clip...it was *my* gun camera! No doubt about it. I jumped up and yelled, "That's my gun camera! George! That's my gun camera!" George shrank down in his chair and said, "Okay, Billy, okay. That's your gun camera. Sit down."

The people in the theater applauded. I took a bow and sat down. "George, you can sit up now. This isn't a scary movie," I said. "Damn! That was my gun camera!"

"Good shooting, Billy," George replied.

NEXT STEPS

When school was out for the summer, Frank or I would drive up to Chicago. We would visit with family and then we would bring Shirley May home for the summer. She would say that it was like visiting her rich relatives. The city girl got to go to the country for the summer.

Soon after we moved to Beatty, we put a garden in. Shirley May would help Thelma can the vegetables from the garden. I would take Richard and Shirley May to a movie or to Young's Dairy in Yellow Springs, Ohio, for some ice cream. Frank and Thelma would also take Shirley May and Richard to the movies and out for a bite to eat.

Life was good. George was married to a real nice girl named Florence—Flo, for short. Those two decided that I needed to settle down. I was for the idea myself. They fixed me up with several girls, but there were no sparks. They got desperate, I guess, and said, "Well, we've got this friend, Phyllis McCauley, but she is divorced and has a small child."

"I'm game," I said, so the date was set and we arranged to meet at a bowling alley.

George and Flo told Phyllis, "He's a little chunky, but we think you'll like him." Unbeknownst to me, Flo and Phyllis had been friends since they were eight years old.

The evening of our date, I shaved, showered, put on some Old Spice, and got dressed before driving to the bowling alley. Phyllis sat in the bowling alley and watched the door. Lucky for me, just before I walked in, a fella who would have made two of me entered.

"Is that him?" Phyllis asked Flo in suppressed horror.

"No," Flo answered. Just then, I came through the door. "That's Bill!" Phyllis relaxed and smiled. Following that fat boy proved to be a great tactical move.

Chester and Beulah McCauley

Phyllis and I hit it off right away. I thought that this was the girl for me. As it turned out, Phyllis had dated a friend of mine, James Kirkendall. I called him on the telephone and told him that Phyllis and I had had a date. I planned to ask her out again, but I didn't want to "beat his time" if there was a chance they might be serious. He said that Phyllis was a great girl. They'd had a few laughs, but there was nothing serious about their relationship.

After that, Phyllis, who I nicknamed Phyl, and I became constant companions. We went to movies, danced, bowled, and played Bridge together. After a while, she introduced me to her son, Larry. He was an ornery little guy and a little awkward. I told Phyl that I wanted to take her and Larry out. She thought that I was a brave man...I told her that we would have fun.

The day of the date I washed and waxed my car. That was not unusual—I was very particular about my car's appearance. I kept my vehicles running like new, clean and polished...inside and out. I drove up to Phyl's parents' house. Phyl waved and smiled as she walked outside. Larry bounced out of the front door. I opened my car door and he piled in the back seat. I greeted Phyl and opened her door for her. We were off.

Billy's parents, Thelma and Frank, in front of Bill and Phyllis's house, Easter late 1950's

We played a round of mini golf. We were thirsty after the golf, so we headed to the root beer stand. I pulled into the parking lot, spotted an open space, and pulled in. A young girl skated up to the car and tried to hand us menus. I told her that we just wanted fries and root beers all around. Our waitress skated up and hung the tray from my car window (the window was rolled up four to six inches to hold the tray). About that time, Larry had to use the restroom. I leaned forward so he could squeeze out the door. I said, "Don't..." That was all I got out. WHAM! He slammed the door. Root beer spilled inside the car, on me, on the seat, dashboard, and down the outside of the door. "Do you have some rags?" I called to our waitress as she turned after hearing the crash.

Phyl also introduced me to her dad, Chet, and her mother, Beulah. Chet was a quiet man with a dry sense of humor. He may have been quiet because Beulah liked to dominate the conversation. She reminded me of Grandma Bailey. Chet was easy to talk to...very down to Earth. He was a bricklayer by trade, and active in his church. Phyl lived at her parents' home with her son. She was an only child, which can be stressful and demanding—especially when your mother is Beulah. Beulah could be caring and sensitive, but she had Phyl running circles trying to please her.

Before long, Phyl and I were in a serious relationship. I remember one time we were playing around in her parents' backyard. I squirted her with a hose. All five foot two of her came at me and gave me a good kick in the shin. Ouch, that smarted! She was a real spitfire, and I loved her. I proposed and she accepted.

Billy D. and Phyllis on their wedding day

Unfortunately, we had to postpone our wedding by a couple of months. I had already used my G.I. Bill to buy a house, so I had to get more money together for a conventional loan. Phyl was not happy, but the day finally came and on June 21, 1952, we were married. Richard was our best man and doubled as the wedding photographer. Phyllis Mae McCauley became Phyl Kasper. Soon after, I went through the process and adopted Larry. His father was never in his life and never protested the adoption.

LEONARD CARTER

After the war, Leonard Carter returned to Clemson University. He graduated in 1948 with a Bachelor of Science in Dairy. He came from a family of farmers, so his degree choice was a natural fit, but the sky called to him. He rejoined the Air Force and signed on as a Flight Instructor. Leonard was assigned to an air base in Georgia. It was close enough that he could return home on the weekends. He fell in love and became engaged to a local girl.

On one particular occasion, he decided to give the town of Ehrhardt, South Carolina, a treat! At first, it sounded like a swarm of bees in the distance. The sound grew louder and closer. One by one, heads turned skyward. Johnny Junior ran to his father and grabbed his hand as he pointed at a fast approaching airplane. "It's Uncle Leonard, Daddy! That's Uncle Leonard in his airplane and he's coming to say hi!"

Most of the Ehrhardt residents looked upward as Leonard made a low pass over the town. As he gained altitude, he said hello by wagging his wings. The plane then shot almost straight up. The engine began to strain as it reached stall speed. It nosed over and the engine roared back to life as he dove down to the deck. The entire town now stood, heads cocked backward, hands cupped over their eyes, to see the private air show over little Ehrhardt. Leonard performed a slow aileron roll. Next, he performed a loop. For his finale, he came in low and fast— inverted. The residents ooohed and aaahed, gasped and clapped. Some, who didn't understand, murmured to one another, "He sure is flashy. He always was a show-off." His detractors didn't understand fighter pilots. Hell, we were all flashy. We learned one way of flying. We were

Captain Billy D. Kasper and 1st Lt. Leonard Carter after their last mission

not bus drivers. Leonard treated his town to an aerial display that most of them would never have had an opportunity to witness.

Later, when the car pulled into the gravel driveway, Johnny ran outside and launched himself into Uncle Leonard's waiting arms. "I saw you flying your plane, Uncle Leonard! That was so neat!"

"I've got something for you, Johnny," Leonard grinned. He revealed a balsa wood airplane for Johnny.

"Thank you," the seven-year-old boy squealed before running off to perform aerobatic maneuvers with the toy plane. Leonard visited with his older brother, Johnny Senior. They ate and laughed and talked about that year's cotton crop. As Leonard was leaving, Johnny Junior launched his plane for another looping flight. The boy took his eye off the plane as he ran to say goodbye to his uncle. He heard the crunching sound under his foot. Johnny's mouth opened wide as he looked down in disbelief. Shock turned to the heartbreak of loss. Tears bubbled up and rolled down his cheeks. He looked at his uncle and wailed, "I've broke it!" Leonard reached down and picked the boy up in his arms. "Don't you cry, Johnny. I'll bring you another one next weekend." The boy's pain soothed, Leonard said his goodbyes and drove off.

Leonard died the following Friday, March 21, 1952. His student pilot from New York lost control of the aircraft and crashed as they attempted to land. Leonard was buried in the family cemetery in Ehrhardt.

FAMILY MATTERS

I told Phyl that I may not be able to have children. Pilots were told that high-altitude flight could cause infertility. I guess they were wrong, because it wasn't too long before Phyl was pregnant. I knew how I wanted to raise my family. I wanted my children to be good, faithful family men or women...honest and dependable. I wanted them to work hard, respect authority, and live by the Golden Rule.

We had our son, Stephen Henry Kasper, on July 27, 1953. We had a scare when Stephen was young. His physical development was on track. The problem was his speech. He had not said a word by the time he turned one year old. The doctor examined him and he couldn't find anything obviously wrong. Stephen seemed mentally alert. The doctor said that he would keep an eye on him and do some research. The months rolled on and the boy did not speak. Could this be some sort of birth defect that resulted from my high-altitude flying? Stephen was approaching his second birthday and still had not spoken. He would smile and laugh, but no words came. Then, when he turned two, he began to speak. After that, we could not shut him up.

I was promoted to foreman, and in 1957, we had another son, Mark David Kasper. He was perfect. We later talked about trying for a girl, but Phyl and I decided that money was tight and we'd probably have another boy, anyway.

Brother Richard was a good student. I asked him if he thought about a military career. He said he had given it some thought. I told him, "Go to the Academy, then." He thought it might be too hard to get in. There are only a few openings every year. I told him to let me see what I could do. I went to see Congressman Clarence Brown Senior, and I championed my brother as a good candidate for West Point. A spot was open for Rich, but he changed his mind and went to Ohio University to study art

Young Sue and Richard

and art education. For his going-away present, I gave him a paint roller and pan.

After he graduated from college, Rich joined the Army. I remember seeing him off to Germany at the train station. Thelma was bawling. I said, "Hell, Mom, it's peacetime. He'll be okay."

Phyl asked, "Did you cry when Bill went off to war?" Phyl knew the answer. I got a big laugh out of that. Thelma just gave me a fiery look and hit me. I laughed again and Thelma turned away and said, "You. Humph."

Richard served his tour. After he came home, he met Sue Weatherhead and settled in Dayton, Ohio. They had a son, Phillip, in 1963. In 1965, they added a daughter, Virginia. Phillip and Virginia were good kids...well-behaved children. On the other hand, my boys were wrestling and fighting every chance they got. Phillip shared my love of cars. It was nice to have something in common with my nephew.

A FAMILIAR FACE

In the early 1960s, Raymond came to Springfield. He was no longer the handsome lady killer. He looked like hell and was penniless. Years of alcohol abuse and unhealthy living had caused his body to bloat. His eyes were puffy. His cheeks sagged and his color was an unhealthy pale hue with purple and red capillaries surfacing on his nose and cheeks. His hair was greasy.

Thelma and Frank ordered him to clean up. I took him out and bought him some clothes. We couldn't really afford it, but Phyl gave me her blessing. He was my uncle, Mom's brother, Shirley May's father. I had to help him.

Frank and Thelma let him stay at their place, but that arrangement didn't last. Raymond got in trouble in a bar downtown. He started a fight. Some men just shouldn't drink. Frank told him he'd have to leave. Thelma gave him some money and that was the last we saw of Raymond. He died a few years later.

LIVING THE DREAM

One year, we bought Larry a game that had a 36-inch-long board as part of the game. He decided to use that board on his brother, Stephen. After that, the board became my paddle. I didn't like disciplining the boys, but I thought discipline and order was important to their growing up.

I enjoyed doing things with the boys. I liked it when we worked on things together. When they were little, they would crawl up in my chair with me, especially Mark, and would stretch out and watch television with me. Mark always liked to be flown into bed at night. "Fly me to bed, Daddy." VROOM! He was my little fighter pilot.

Unfortunately, it wasn't long before Stephen began having trouble seeing the board at school. We took him to the eye doctor and he came home with a prescription for glasses. Mark went to the eye doctor when he was eight years old and also came home with an eyeglass prescription. There would be no pilots in this family.

We got along just fine, though. Larry entered The Ohio State University and studied Business. I continued to get promotions. I ran different departments as a foreman, and was promoted to supervisor. Over the years, I was a supervisor in charge of different areas of the shop

We had a good family life. One of my only regrets was that I should have put cotton in my ears when I was a pilot...and as I worked around and tested engines. Now, at this point in my life, I had to turn up the television to hear the programs. Hearing aids were inevitable. Hindsight is 20/20.

Our neighborhood was alive with young families. There were children all around. Within a five-house radius there were at least 25 children. The kids, weather permitting, were always outside playing. When it was time for the children to come home for a meal or for the evening, the calls went out. Several methods were used to call the children home. One mother called her children with a police whistle. One father used the two-fingered-whistle method. Another father used the protruding lower jaw, curled tongue whistle. One mother rang a cowbell. One family had enough money to afford wristwatches for their kids. My method was my big mouth. The boys could be blocks away and hear my call.

We had a neighbor, Chuck, who worked third shift. His wife called Phyl and told her that when I called the boys home, Chuck would sit straight up in bed. He would be so startled that he had trouble returning to sleep. Sorry, Chuck.

The only repairman we ever had in the house was a television repair-man. That was the one repair that I didn't tackle. I fixed the plumbing and electrical. Steve or Mark would hand me tools and work with me. They would also help me work on the car. I think Mark helped the most. I can remember lying on our gravel driveway with Mark, dropping the transmission from our 1963 Ford Fairlane. I thought he might become an engineer, but the boys never really took to working with me in the same way as I did with Frank. They would help, but they didn't ask the probing questions. They just wanted to get whatever had broken fixed as quickly as possible. I don't think they wanted to really dive into the workings of the machine. That was all right. They would have to find their own way.

As the kids got older, we put an above-ground pool in the yard. I didn't use it much, as I had never cared for the water. It was okay to look at and I liked listening to a babbling mountain creek. The only time I wanted in it, though, was when I took a shower.

We were also blessed enough to be able to take a vacation every year. In 1967, we went to the Expo in Montréal. The kids got to see exhibits from all over the world. America's pavilion was very disappointing. Raggedy Ann Dolls. Dolls everywhere. Who the hell's idea was that?

I remembered the Chicago World Fair. We had great exhibits there that showed America's technical and industrial achievements. In Montréal, the

United States displayed dolls. How disappointing. The rest of the Expo was impressive. The kids also got to ride their first subway. On our return trip, we stopped at Niagara Falls. We put on rain suits, rode an elevator down to a man-made tunnel, and stood behind the falls. That was quite a sight. Millions of gallons of water rushed over the rocks to the river below.

It honestly didn't take much to entertain me. I liked going to car lots and looking. Sometimes, I test drove, but usually I just liked to look and talk cars. Phyl and I would also play Bridge with friends, and we took the boys to a few Reds games. We went to the Wright Patterson Air Force Museum about once every two years, and would go the Dayton Air Show and to the county fair. Every Sunday, we would visit Frank and Thelma in Beatty.

Chet and Beulah lived two blocks away. They would visit Phyl a couple times a week. At Christmas, we would drive to Dayton and Columbus to shop in the department stores. The kids liked riding the escalators. Most of all, I just enjoyed being at home with my family. I guess I was always just a homebody at heart.

As I mentioned, I liked cars. In the mid to late 1960s, we got to a point that we could afford a second car. I used this as an opportunity to play. I bought a different second car every other year or so. One time, I bought a little red Renault. Unfortunately, I discovered that on a snowy, icy day, when a Renault takes on a fire hydrant...the fire hydrant wins big. I also had a black Mercury Monarch. One fella at work thought I worked for the mob. I told him I had my eye on him. I had a red Trans Am with a black eagle on the hood. Driving that car was almost like flying. When I sold it, Phyl wouldn't talk to me for a week. I guess she really liked that car, too. I always thought, have your fun and then move on.

I liked to play around. Not with girls—one is enough—but with engines and things mechanical. I once bought an old broken-down motorcycle. I tore it down, rebuilt it, and sold it. I rode it once and that was enough. Buying and trading cars was a great hobby. I also liked guns. I would go to gun shows and buy guns or just look. I didn't have a big gun collection, just a few pieces that I liked.

One thing I didn't like was talking about the war—something I didn't do except with my family. If someone asked, I would tell them that I had fought in WWII. If they would press me for details, I would tell them that that was a long time ago. Next subject. I didn't talk about it—not because of deep scars or anything like that. I just didn't want to sound like I was tooting my own horn. I did my job, just like a lot of men did. Someone once asked me how I be-came a captain at the age of

Bill, Frank, and Richard

21. I told them that I got promoted because so many of our boys were get-ting killed that they decided to promote me. Kind of a flippant answer, but I didn't want to brag. A lot of good men fought and died in that war.

I told my boys, "If you ever play with a child whose father works at the shop, make sure you say, 'My dad works with your dad'...not 'Your dad works for my dad.'" I don't think I would have blistered their bottom for saying it the other way, but I would have been very disappointed.

In 1968, Mark and I began an annual trek to the Indy time trials. We had a great time. Richard's son, Phillip, joined us a few years later. A couple years after that, Richard started coming with us. We went to the time trials and races until 1985. All things must come to an end.

TRANSITIONS

In 1969, Frank retired from the shop. He was excited about working his garden. He worked around the house and spent more time with Thelma. When he was home, he might be found working in the garden, work-ing around the house, or working on his car. He and Thelma went to the Kentucky Derby and drank mint juleps. They took Phillip and Virginia on little camping trips. They enjoyed retirement. Mom and Dad enjoyed the simple pleasures of life. They worked in their garden and canned the fruits of their labors. They would sit in their straight-back chairs with the table between them and read their papers and magazines. Frank and Thelma enjoyed each other's company and they enjoyed life with one another. The simplest pleasures are the best. I learned that at a young age. The war reinforced my beliefs. So did my 1970 birthday present.

The day before my birthday, Phyl and I had dinner at home alone. Larry was in Michigan working on his MBA. Steve and Mark had gone to a movie. At about 9:00 pm, the boys came home. They walked in the door, holding a puppy. Not just a puppy—an Airedale. "Happy Birthday," Phyl, Steve, and Mark said.

I got down on the floor and petted that little dog. I held his head and looked at him. We called him Alexander. Seeing him brought back a lot of good memories. I thought of Grandpa's Airedale. It had been almost 40 years since Grandpa and his Airedale died. I loved my grandpa's dog.

Alexander grew into a fine dog. He was loyal and quicker than a rabbit—literally. He caught more than one that wandered into the yard. After he caught the rabbit he would toss it up in the air. It would land, unmoving, and Alexander would look at it as if it were a sore sport for not playing anymore.

Alexander had a little friend who lived in the house behind us. She was a 20-pound black-and-white terrier. The little dog would run the fence with Alexander, barking as it ran. The dog had a voice box problem, and its bark sounded something like an abbreviated seal's bark. Friends would visit us. If we were in the backyard, we would hear the little dog's "Arf." A curious look would come over our friends' faces when they first heard the bark. They would cock their heads and then scan the yard with their eyes, searching for the source of the odd sound. Their eyes would locate the barking terrier and they would howl with laughter.

One day, the phone rang and Phyl answered. It was our neighbor who owned the little terrier. "Phyl," she cried.

"Yes, Betty?"

"Can you do something about that dog of yours?"

"What do you mean, Betty?"

"Your dog keeps peeing on my dog's head. Every day, I have to give her a bath. I'm just at my wits end."

"Betty, I don't know what I can do. Dogs sniff and pee. I can't stand at the back door to make sure Alexander doesn't pee on your dog. What do you want me to do?"

Crying, Betty said, "Could you call your dog in when I let mine out?"

"I'll try, Betty. I'm terribly sorry."

Phyl tried to keep an eye on Alexander, but dogs will do what dogs do.

October 28, 1970, the phone rang. I answered. It was bad news. My old friend, James Kirkendall, had died in a traffic accident. He left behind a wife and two children. Hanging up the phone my thoughts drifted back to the summer of 1965. Phyl, the kids, and I were driving home on Route 40. The next thing I knew, a patrol car was behind me with his lights and siren on. I pulled over. I didn't think I was speeding. As I rolled down the window and reached for my wallet, I heard a familiar voice. "Hi, Billy," laughed Jim Kirkendall. "I saw you and thought I'd just say hello." We had a nice talk. Phyl and I would miss him.

Another bit of sad news came to us on May 30, 1973; Thelma called early in the morning. She was at the hospital with Frank. He woke up and was throwing-up blood. Phyl and I rushed to the hospital. Stephen had taken time off from college. He was working third shift in the foundry at Cooper Energy. He came into the hospital, black-sand bootprints following him to the waiting area. Mark was asleep in bed at home. The doctors took Frank in for emergency surgery. He had had an aneurism in his stomach. The doctor came out. Frank didn't make it. He was dead.

Phyl and I drove home. I had worked with that man since I was a young boy. He was my father, my friend. I cried. It was the only time Phyl ever saw me cry. I think it was the first time I had cried since I was a small boy and skinned my knee. We buried Frank at Glen Haven Cemetery.

After that, Richard, the boys, and I would help out in the yard and around Mom's house. The house seemed empty. I remembered the times that, early in the morning, Frank and I would sit together in the kitchen. We would drink our coffee and have a cigarette before we would go to work. Later, after I was married, we would sit at that same table on Sundays and talk shop, cars, or about this and that. Mom and Frank had cigarettes with their coffee or while they sat and read. Smoking was a shared experience.

Thelma took up smoking after we buried Grandma Bailey. We all wondered if it was because she feared the wrath of her mother. Interestingly enough, she quit after Frank died. A year later, Ma sold the house in Beatty and moved into a mobile home park.

It's entirely possible Frank's death set Beulah and Chet to thinking, because it wasn't long before they bought burial plots. They also bought two plots for Phyl and me. Four plots in a row, situated near Frank and Thelma's plots. It was a nice gesture.

Traditionally, as you look down on a grave, the husband is on the left and the wife is on the right. Since Beulah had purchased the plots, she had decided that I would be between her and Phyl. In other words: Chet, Beulah, Bill, Phyl. Phyl got a hold of the manager of the cemetery and told him, "Bill is *not* going to spend eternity next to my mother. You will put *me* next to Mother." Chet, Beulah, Phyl, and Bill.

The manager protested. "We can't put the man on the right," he said.

Phyl replied, "Bill has been a good son-in-law, but it would not be fair for him to have to rest beside her." So, the plots were rearranged. I had no idea. Thanks, Phyl

Even amidst all the death and cemetery business, life went on. Larry married Helen Harrison in 1976. He told her that she had to promise not to have children. She did and they didn't.

Stephen and Mark grew more and more ornery. One Sunday, I was sitting in my recliner, watching a preseason football game. Stephen was seated to my left. Mark was seated to my right. Out of the corner of my eyes I could see that they were exchanging looks. They were up to something. I was on alert. My attention slowly returned to the game. I hardly noticed as the boys stood up in unison. Suddenly, they lunged at me. Stephen pinned my left arm and Mark pinned my right arm. Before I could react, they licked my arms from elbow to wrist. They quickly released my arms and stepped back. "Oooooooo!" I said. "What the hell? Yuck! You stupes!" The boys howled. I wiped my arms. "You silly shits! You! Oooo!" The boys roared with laughter. They got the old man. Mission accomplished.

Over the next couple weeks they sprung a few more sneak attacks. One late summer day I was watching a football game. Mark was lying on the couch and Stephen sat next to me, watching the game. They stood up and asked if I wanted a drink. "No. I'm fine," I replied. They sprang at me. I didn't move. They grabbed my arm. I smiled. Their tongues traced my forearm. They came up sputtering and spitting. "Ohh! Yuck! Stplaaa!" It was my turn. I roared with laughter.

Earlier, before the game, I had been working in the yard. I had a sneaking suspicion an attack was imminent. It was 80 degrees outside and I had worked up quite a sweat.

Billy D. on the wing of a P51

Normally, I would have showered and cleaned up. Today, after working in the yard, I just toweled off and changed my shirt. When Mark and Stephen gave my arm that big lick, they got a mouth full of dried, salty sweat. That was the end of the sneak attacks. They may have won a few battles, but the old man won the war.

Speaking of war, in 1976, Phyl and I went to an 8th Air Force Reunion in England. As we traveled to East Wretham, I described the manor to Phyl. I was looking forward to introducing her to some of my old friends. When we arrived at the old base, there was an empty, weed-filled spot where that grand manor hall had stood. It had burned down in 1949.

As the day went on, I learned that many of my old friends were already dead. Oh, brother. We still had a good time. The Brits were good hosts. I did get to talk old times with the men who were still alive. It was interesting to watch the pilots with the old planes. The bomber pilots and crews would affectionately walk around and touch the B-17 that was on display. They acted like they had just seen their long-lost mother who had nursed and cared for them all those years ago. On the other hand, there were the P-51 pilots. We climbed around and slid into the cockpit of the P-51s on display. We acted like we were just reunited with a wild old lover—and the sex was good.

BUSINESS AS USUAL

Steve graduated college and a couple years later, he moved to Dallas, Texas. Phyl and I would miss Stephen, but a man has to do what's best for himself. We knew we would make the best of it and take trips to Dallas. A good reason to travel.

Back at work, National Supply became White Motors, which became Cooper Energy. I stayed at the shop and continued to advance. I was promoted to factory manager. I was responsible for the product from the time it left the foundry until the finished product was shipped. I never talked too much about work at home. When I came home, I just wanted to be home.

The most unpleasant part of being a manager was firing someone. Phyl always knew when I was going to fire a foreman or supervisor. I would wash dishes. I would wash the hell out of those dishes. I found dish washing to be—well, therapeutic. I used bleach in the dishwater.

Back then, plastic was a newer alternative to glass and ceramic. Plastic was a durable non-breakable product. I went to the store one day and bought two liters of Pepsi. I called Phyl to look at the new design of the bottle. I dropped a two-liter bottle. Phyl's eyes bulged. The bottle hit the floor and she shrieked. The bottle bounced. A new plastic bottle. Phyl didn't think the bouncing bottle was as funny as I did. Unfortunately, plastic cups and glasses did have a drawback...they retained the strong bleach smell from my dishwashing. Phyl and the kids never complained, though.

Sometimes, I would get a call at home from a foreman's wife, asking me to give her husband another chance. That was hard. I never took the firing of a person lightly. After a man lost his job, the whole family suffered. I would tell the man's wife, "I didn't fire your husband for what happened yesterday. I fired him for all the things he did or didn't do all the other yesterdays." I felt bad for the wife, but the bottom line was, I didn't let her family down.

Phyl wanted me to tell two stories about work. In the sixties, Joe Meyers was the factory manager. Joe had a way of wearing his anger on his sleeve. He had a temper and didn't mind using it. Once a week, Joe had a meeting with his supervisors. One particular meeting, he was on a roll. Joe stood at the front of the room and ranted...then, he asked for input. He got no reply. He yelled some more and asked for ideas; no reply. The meeting continued like this until, finally, he raised his arms and yelled, "Why the hell doesn't anybody say anything!?" The room was quiet. You could have heard a pin drop. "Well?" he yelled. The room stayed quiet. I finally had to open my big mouth, "Joe, no one has anything to say because no matter what we say you will just yell. No one has the right answer for you today." There was a long pause. Then Joe said, "Meeting dismissed." I liked Joe. We got along and worked well together. Joe was also a good friend to Frank. He was a pallbearer at Frank's funeral.

On another day, I was walking the departments and heard a V12 on the test stand start. Immediately, the sound of the engine rose to a loud clatter. "Runaway engine!" A person can work around engines for 40 years and never experience a runaway. The throttle and the governor control the revolutions per minute (RPM)

Billy D. (center) at "The Shop"

of an engine. When these controls fail, the engine revs higher and higher. The RPMs scream faster and faster, and if not stopped, the engine will fly apart. With engines the size of the ones we built back then—well, someone could get killed. When I heard it, I took off running toward the engine. I grabbed up a pipe wrench as I ran to the steel fuel line and struck the steel line over and over and over until the engine gasped and stopped. The only way to stop a runaway engine is to starve it. No big deal.

In 1978, my Airedale died. In 1979, Stephen found another Airedale in Texas and shipped the dog to Dayton. Once again, I had an Airedale. His name was Sampson. He wasn't the fast rabbit dog that Alexander had been, but he was a good boy. He was a lap dog. When I would sit down to

Sampson on Billy D.'s lap

watch television, he'd hop up in my lap and recline with me in my Lazy Boy chair. We no longer had small children, so he sort of became my little boy. He died in 1992. I had had a dog since I was a small boy. When Sampson died, though, that was it for me. No more dogs.

July 25, 1981, Phyl's father, Chet, died. Chet's health had been failing for a few years. He told Phyl that he'd hang on as long as he could. He was all that stood between Phyl and Beulah...the "buffer," so to speak. Chet was 83 years old. He had been a good father-in-law and a kind, gentle man. He had a dry sense of humor. Not only was he a good father-in-law, he was a good husband, father, and family man.

Honestly, there was nothing like the death of a family member to put other things in perspective. Mark wasn't focused and didn't know what he wanted to do, so he left college and got a job in the foundry. All three of the boys worked at Cooper at one time or another. Larry worked one summer between high school and college. Steve worked for a year when he took some time off from college. Mark worked three years in the foundry. I liked the thought of three generations of Kaspers having worked at the shop. Most of all, though, I wanted the boys to get a college education.

In 1985, all of them finally did finish their education. Mark was a little slow, but he graduated. That same year, he married Kathy Gracy. At the wedding rehearsal dinner, I gave a toast. "Happy Life." It was a simple toast...a toast that sums up my wish for my children. Happy Life. Maintain a good attitude and positive approach to life. A person will have a happy life—if they truly want one. Happy Life.

In the early 1980s, Cooper's engine business declined. Mark was laid off and went back to school. By the mid-1980s, the foundry was closed. Its business was shipped to an existing foundry in Mount Vernon, Ohio. The workforce was reduced at the shop, because higher-ups wanted to further decrease expenses. They told me to lay off this supervisor, then that supervisor, and so on. I had to lay off men I'd known for 25 to 35 years. I had no choice. It didn't matter how good of a worker the fella was. I followed orders. Some men understood; some men would never speak to me again.

Springfield was also in a deep decline. In the 1940s, it was ranked as the number four fastest-growing industrial town...number four in the whole country. The population rose to around 80,000 people by the 1960s. Then, it shrank to about 60,000 and counting. Like

Billy D. with his three sons Steve, Larry, and Mark

so many prosperous cities, the leaders of Springfield did not look for to the future. They did not create a town that would welcome the 21st century. Springfield began to look and act tired—like a dying old man. The writing was on the wall. In 1987, I was laid off (retired). I was 63.

People make a lot of plans. Retirement at age 63 was not part of my plan. Phyl and I had a budget laid out into our retirement years. Retiring two years early changed our plans. I guess I had some friends in upper-level management. About one year after I was "retired," I was asked to do some consulting. I agreed and consulted on and off for a couple of years. The money from the consulting did help.

After I was retired I found a Toyota in Columbus, Ohio, that had thrown a rod. I drove to Columbus, purchased the car, and towed it to my garage. I tore that engine down and rebuilt it. That was my idea of fun. It was my hobby. I drove that Toyota for a year, then I sold it.

GENERATIONS TO COME

On April 13, 1987, Mark and Kathy had our first grandchild, Derek David Kasper. When your children have children, it's a wonderful thing. Seeing your child with their child brings back all those memories of when they were born. I can't describe the feeling when I first saw that little man.

After Mark and Kathy went back to work, we watched Derek on Wednesdays. Wednesdays became "Derek Days." On August 11, 1988, Mark and Kathy had Blake Alexander Kasper. Soon, Wednesdays became "Derek and Blake Days." The pace of everyday life picked up again.

Mom's activity level, on the other hand, had all but ceased by the mid-1980s. She stayed in her mobile home, except when Richard and I or the kids would take her shopping or out for a meal. Mom bought a bird for company. She would talk to it and teach it to say a word or two. After about a year, the bird died. We bought another—it died a couple months later. We bought another and it died. We figured that Mom would grab the bird and simply squeeze too tight, so we stopped replacing the birds.

In early 1989, Mom fell in her bathroom and couldn't get up. Richard and I were forced to put her in a nursing home. Within a couple of months, her health failed completely. I remember we were called in to say goodbye. She had the death rattle, but she didn't die.

Two days later, Phyl and I were by her side. It was July 6, 1989. The death rattle continued. Phyl looked at me and said, "Tell her you love her, Bill."

"She knows that."

Phyl repeated, "Just tell her, Bill."

I bent down and spoke into her ear, "Mom, it's Bill. I love you. You can let go now."

A few minutes later, Mom died.

They say where one life ends, another begins. In 1990, Mark and Kathy had a daughter, Erika Marie. She was born on my birthday and I couldn't have asked for a better present. Phyl finally got her girl. She had wanted a girl in the family for years. Now she had a little girl that she could "do girl things with."

After I retired, Phyl and I took about two vacations a year. One of them would be a trip to Texas to visit Stephen. In 1990, he met and married Jenny Eiden. Phyl and I traveled to Texas for the wedding.

I had quit smoking in the 1960s. Unfortunately, my friend George Gibson did not. He was diagnosed with lung cancer and had surgery, but he continued smoking. He would sneak outside and have a cigarette. He wasn't fooling Flo. After an extended illness, he returned to the hospital to die. I tried to visit George every day. He had been a good friend through the years. Besides Phyl, he was my best friend. On January 28, 1993, George died.

Time marched on. Mark and Kathy had number four on April 24, 1993—a boy and named Grant McCauley Kasper. On Wednesdays, Phyl and I sure had a houseful of little ones. I'd take the kids around on the riding mower with the blades off. We would play games. The kids would get into the cabinets and concoct drinks and make interesting food "recipes." Of course, grandma and grandpa were the food critics. Every dish and drink was delicious.

We also grew pumpkins in the backyard. When Derek was a little guy, I sat him down in the highchair at the kitchen table and carved a pumpkin with him. From that point on, pumpkin carving with the grandkids became a tradition.

Naturally, when the grandchildren came along, we bought a video camera. The first time I used it, I didn't record a damned thing. Operator error. When the machine was recording properly, a red light was illuminated. The operator couldn't see the red light, but the person being taped could see it.

Around our house, the refrain when I was filming was, "Is the red light on? Is the light on?"

"Yes, Bill, the light is on."

"Is the light on?"

"Yes, Dad, the light's on?"

"Is the light on?"

"Yes, Grandpa, the light is on." Giggle. Giggle. Giggle.

The grandkids would crawl up with me in my chair. We would stretch out and talk about things or just relax. Sometimes, I'd turn on a movie for the kids—a good John Wayne or Clint Eastwood movie. We also enjoyed watching "Top Gun." I bought the movie and would fast-forward past the racy parts. We also watched "The Right Stuff." The kids would say, "Grandpa, you got the Right Stuff."

I replied, "You say I'm full of stuff."

They laughed and repeated, "You've got the Right Stuff." That was real sweet of the kids. I think they were a little prejudiced for grandpa. Of course who wouldn't be...especially when I started sneezing.

One... two... three. The grandkids giggled. Four... five. They rolled about on the floor as they laughed. Six... "One more, Grandpa!" They giggled. Seven!!! The kids loved to count my sneezes. I always sneezed seven

Grandpa Billy with Derek

Grandpa Billy with Blake

Grandpa Billy with Grant

Grandpa Billy with Kayla

Grandpa Billy with Erika and Hana

times. I don't know why, I just did.

On October 7, 1993, Steve and Jenny had a daughter, Hannah Mae Kasper. Phyl and I now had another reason to visit Texas.

On October 29, 1994, Mark and Kathy had their fifth child. Her name was Kayla Quinn Kasper. I was a grandpa six times over. We continued to have the kids on Wednesdays.

In 1998, Mark took a new job and was transferred to Lima, Ohio. Our Wednesdays were over. We made the best of it. Nothing lasts forever. Phyl and I would drive to Lima about once a month. We'd spend two or three days at a time in Lima. Phyl and I could never be gone more than a couple days. Beulah would raise a fuss when we left Springfield for very long. Phyl was all she had and she made sure her mother's needs were tended to.

When Beulah could no longer take care of herself, she went kicking and screaming into a nursing home. Phyl couldn't take care of her, but she visited her mother practically every day. She did all she could to make sure that Beulah got the best care possible. Beulah never appreciated all that Phyl did for her.

FINAL BATTLE

It was around 1998 that I started having problems. I would forget things. I couldn't keep events in sequence. One time, I drove to a park in Springfield. I couldn't remember how I got there. I knew something was wrong. I knew I might be in trouble. I was diagnosed with Alzheimer's disease. Alzheimer's is a slow, creeping, cruel disease that is terminal. It robs the brain of its connections to reality, recognition, and the joy of life.

In the early stages, I was pretty good at covering up the disease. By that, I mean if Phyl would mention something that had happened the previous day, I would say, "Oh, yes, now I remember." I didn't, but I would go along. Go with the flow. Yes, I knew I had Alzheimer's, but by the time I knew it, it didn't really sink in. I drove and functioned pretty normally until mid-2001.

In February of 2001, Phyl and I went to Detroit to visit Mark and Kathy and the kids. We drove to the Henry Ford Museum. As we walked through the exhibits, we heard a piano playing dance music from the 1940s. We

Phyllis and Billy D. with family on 50th wedding anniversary.
Front Row left to right: Jenni, Erika, Derek, Kathy
Middle Row left to right: Hannah, Steve, Kayla, Mark, Grant
Back Row left to right: Helen, Larry, Phyllis, Bill, Blake

walked into the hall with its wood floor and high ceiling. I led Phyl by the hand to within 10 feet of the piano. We always held hands. I faced Phyl. The old twinkle was in my eyes as I looked at her. I took her in my arms and we glided across the floor. I will never forget that day. When the music stopped playing, Mark and Kathy and the kids applauded and we took our bow.

In October of 2001, Mark and Kathy bought a campground in Granville, Ohio. Phyl drove us to visit them. My eyes still had a sparkle. Early in the disease, the eyes have a questioning look. We are trying to figure out what the hell is going on. The mind is trying to make sense of the world. When you look into the eyes of a person with advanced Alzheimer's, the eyes are empty. We might appear to be daydreaming, lost in thought. Maybe the fire within me or stubbornness or who knows what helped me fight the disease. It's a losing battle.

Phyl bought a Park model camper at Mark and Kathy's campground. She had hoped I would like camping. We had camped a lot when the kids were young. Her plan didn't work so well. I would be ready to go back home in short order. That is a part of the disease. The ill person's world gets smaller and smaller.

Larry would come over from Columbus. He would take me out for drives or maybe to see a movie. As time went on, I wasn't interested in movies or television. One time, Larry took me to the Springfield Airport to see jets from the Air National Guard fly in and land. I really enjoyed that.

Steve, Jenni, and Hannah came up from Texas in June of 2002 to visit and help Phyl around the house. It was also Phyl's and my 50th wedding anniversary. The whole family had a nice dinner at Mark and Kathy's. When Steve left, he took my guns with him. Probably a wise move. One of the most difficult things to deal with was not driving. I still wanted to drive my car. I could get pretty damned demanding. No car keys for Bill.

August 25, 2003, Erika went to the nursing home with Phyl to see Beulah, whose health was failing. Not long after they returned from the visit; the nursing home called and told us that Beulah had died. Phyl's folks and my folks were now gone. My disease progressed.

One day, Phyl and I were out shopping. Standing near us in an aisle was a gentleman. He was about six feet two, medium build, and in his early sixties. I faced him and said hello. He gave me one of those curt grunts and turned his body so it wasn't facing me. I continued to try to make polite conversation. I was smiling. I didn't have a "your ass needs kicked" look on my face. That fella just turned and took a few steps away. At that point, I stopped talking and my smile disappeared. I wonder if he thought the Alzheimer's would rub off on him. I looked at Phyl, shrugged, and said, "Oh well."

Phyl said, "Wait here, Bill." All five feet two of her walked over to that guy and she proceeded to dress him down like a lowly recruit at boot camp. I think if he'd had said a word back, she would have come out swinging. Don't think she wouldn't. When she was in high school, three girls tried to bully her as she walked home. She whooped them all right there. Then she felt bad because as she found out later, one of the girls had a limp from polio.

183

After Phyl finished with that gentleman, my little spitfire and I headed out to have lunch. I enjoyed eating out with Phyl and taking walks at the mall. She's a good girl.

In early 2005, I was at Mark's house. I guess he sensed something. He looked me in the eye and said, "Are you ready to be with God, Dad."

"I'm ready, son." He hugged and kissed me. A lot of people might not think I knew what I was saying at that moment, but I always said people will believe what they want to believe. Mark knew.

Billy D. sitting alone at the Lazy River Campground

Phyl and I returned home from lunch one day in February. She got my coat off and hung it up. Phyl said, "Bill, do you hear something?"

"Nope."

"I hear something," she repeated. She walked to the basement door and walked downstairs. Now I heard something. "Bill," she yelled. "Water is gushing all over the basement."

I saw the water gushing. There was so much water it was hard to tell where it was coming from. Something inside me clicked. I ran to the gushing water and identified which pipe was broken. I located the shut-off valve for that pipe and turned off the water. Boy, was I soaked. I guess I had just performed one last hurrah.

People with Alzheimer's can perform activities such as dancing, but not toward the conclusion of the disease. I played Bridge and won until early 2005. I had worked with my hands all my life, but now I needed help getting dressed. Hell, I couldn't find the bathroom. Sometimes I couldn't open a door. But on this day, I knew exactly what to do. What do you know?

On March 23, 2005, I was running errands with Phyl. When I attempted to get into the car, I fell down. I couldn't get up and Phyl couldn't get me up. At that point in time, I didn't know how to get up. I was lost. I couldn't even speak. Phyl had to call an ambulance. I went into a nursing home and never left. They placed me on a rolling hospital bed. I was in a common area of the Alzheimer's floor. I didn't speak. I was in sort of a cata-tonic state. Phyl, Mark, Kathy, Derek, Blake, Erika, Grant, and Kayla sat and

stood around me. They held my hands and talked quietly to me. Derek couldn't hold it in any longer. He cried. I couldn't even hug him.

Eventually, I rallied. I could talk to Phyl and the people around me. I could feed myself with a little help. But I couldn't go home. This would be my last home.

Billy D. and Phyllis on a boat in Wyandotte, Michigan

Paul Harvey used to do a segment on his program called, "The Rest of the Story." The real hero of my story is my best friend, Phyllis Mae McCauley Kasper. When I was in the deepest throws of Alzheimer's, she took care of me. She was there for me every day. She was there for me when I needed someone the most. She kept me with her in our home as long as she could. The familiar surround-ings of our home were a comfort to me. There were so many people from so many quarters who wanted me in a nursing home. They said, "We are thinking of you, Phyl. We don't want you to suffer or die from the physical and mental strain of taking care of Bill." Well-meaning people who didn't have a clue of the depth of our love. They didn't—couldn't—fathom the connection that we still had. Everyone should be half as lucky as I was. Phyl was my lifeline. She was strong when I needed her the most. Up until the very end, I knew Phyl. She was always there for me. Our love connec-tion was strong until the end. Even Alzheimer's couldn't come between our love for each other. Phyllis Mae McCauley Kasper was my hero. Who is yours?

AFTERWORD

A HERO

Shirley May Bailey Keifer told me, "If it wasn't for Frank and Billy, I wouldn't have known there were good men in this world." Heroes are in the right place at the right time and do the right thing. Most heroes are everyday people. They are moms who bandage a cut and soothe a crying child. Heroes are big brothers and sisters who take younger siblings to a movie or help them with homework. A hero can be a hero by simply living an ordinary life.

I could set my clock by my father. He would be home for lunch at 11:37 am. He would be home for dinner at 5:07 pm. When I was a child, I felt a little taller, a little stronger when I was with my father. When I was a grown man, I hugged and kissed him every time I was with him. I am not half the man he was. As an adult, I matured and appreciated the man. I was fortunate to have my dad as long as I did.

On September 23, 2005, six months to the day from entering the nursing home, my father died in his sleep. His room was decorated with family pictures, the American flag, and a picture of a P-51. He had a good life and a good family. He had a Happy Life. The sad thing about heroes is that they leave us. The great thing about heroes is that they were a part of our lives.

Billy D. Kasper was my hero.

Mark D. Kasper

Phyl, Mark, and Billy D.

About The Author

Mark Kasper graduated from Wright State University and currently lives in Granville, Ohio with his wife, Kathy. They have five children and own and operate a campground called Lazy River at Granville.

Please visit our website

WWW.LAZYRIVERATGRANVILLE.COM

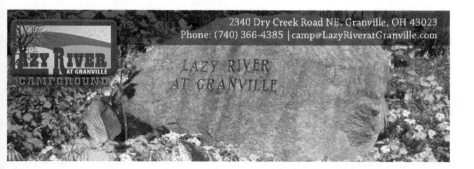

2340 Dry Creek Road NE, Granville, OH 43023
Phone: (740) 366-4385 | camp@LazyRiveratGranville.com

LAZY RIVER
AT GRANVILLE

CPSIA information can be obtained
at www.ICGtesting.com
Printed in the USA
FFOW03n1110110217
32184FF

9 780578 105215